Front cover: Typical motive power on the route was the 5100 class 2-6-2T. No. 5167 waits at Much Wenlock with a train from Wellington on 31st August 1959. (F.Hornby)

Back cover: The Buildwas-Lightmoor section was retained for coal traffic via Madeley to Ironbridge 'B' Power Station. No. 66091 is on Coalbrookdale Viaduct in June 2003. (P.Jones)

Published August 2008

ISBN 978 1 906008 33 8

© Middleton Press, 2008

Design Deborah Esher
Typesetting Barbara Mitchell

Published by
 Middleton Press
 Easebourne Lane
 Midhurst
 West Sussex
 GU29 9AZ
Tel: 01730 813169
Fax: 01730 812601
Email: info@middletonpress.co.uk
www.middletonpress.co.uk

Printed & bound by Biddles Ltd, Kings Lynn

INDEX

80-81 Madeley Branch

54	Buildwas		
67	Coalbrookdale	85 Horsehay & Dawley	34 Much Wenlock
1	Craven Arms	101 Ketley	98 New Dale Halt
83	Doseley Halt	99 Ketley Town Halt	29 Presthope
28	Easthope Halt	95 Lawley Bank	15 Rushbury
52	Farley Halt	75 Lightmoor Platform	89 Telford Steam Railway
73	Greenbank Halt	20 Longville	106 Wellington
10	Harton Road	80 Madeley Salop	33 Westwood Halt
			8 Wistanstow Halt

ACKNOWLEDGEMENTS

We are very grateful for the assistance received from many of those mentioned in the credits also to D.Angell, W.R.Burton, A.R.Carder, P.Coutanche, L.Crosier, G.Croughton, N.Langridge, B.Lewis, D.T.Rowe, Mr D. and Dr S.Salter, M.Turvey and in particular our wives Barbara Mitchell and Janet Smith.

I. Railway Clearing House map for 1947, with halts added.

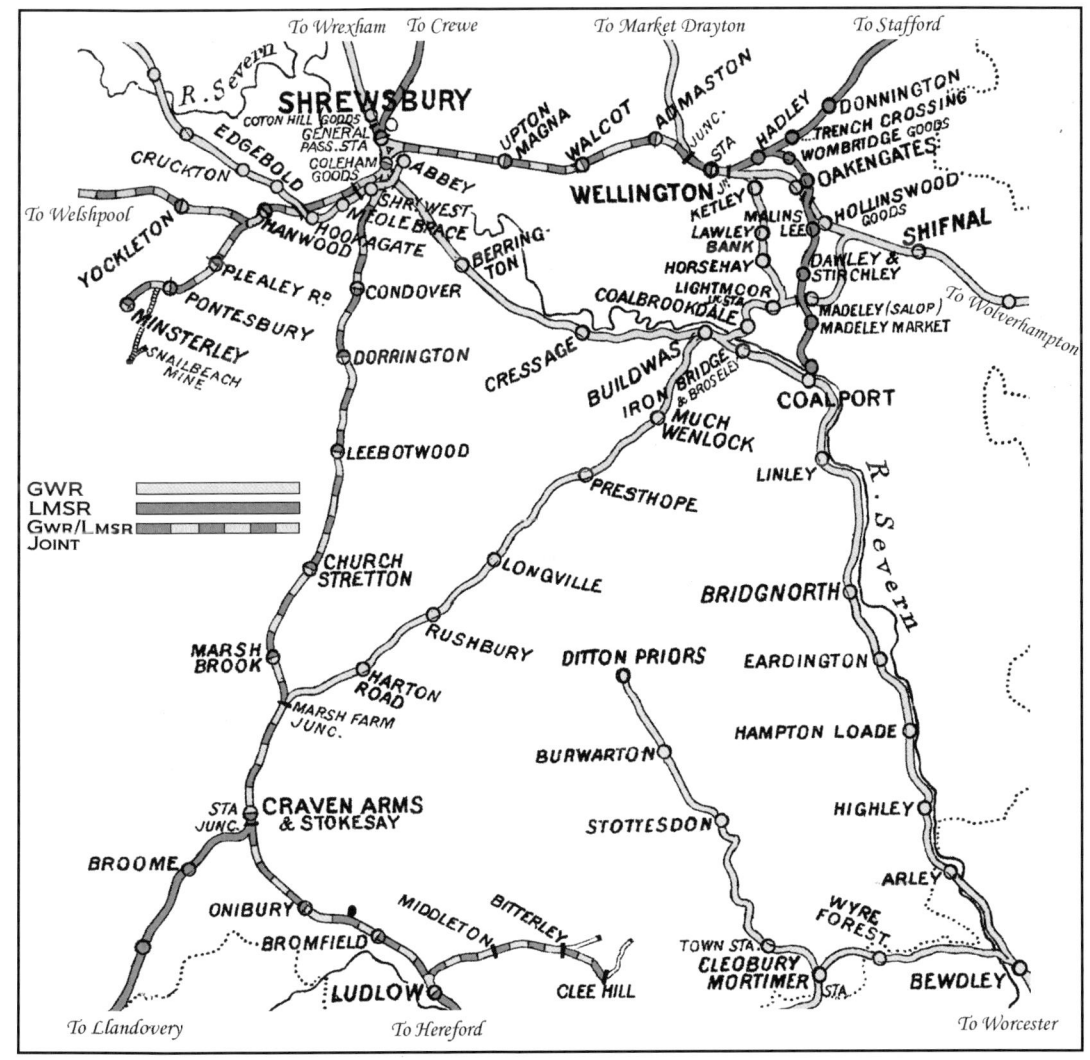

GEOGRAPHICAL SETTING

The route between Craven Arms and Buildwas is at the foot of Wenlock Edge and is roughly parallel to this impressive outcrop of Limestone. The line climbs close to a small watercourse for about seven miles and reaches the watershed near Longville. A descent follows to enter the Severn Valley at Buildwas.

The remainder of the journey is over complex geology, which includes ironstone and coal, once of economic value. These were commodities which helped Wellington to become Shropshire's second town. The entire route was in that county and ran through agricultural countryside south of Buildwas. Many of the gradients north thereof were at 1 in 40 through the East Shropshire Coalfield.

All the places between Coalbrookdale and Wellington have been incorporated into Telford, the New Town process starting in 1968.

The maps are to the scale of 25ins to 1 mile, with north at the top, unless otherwise indicated.

HISTORICAL BACKGROUND

Our route runs between the 1852 Shrewsbury & Hereford Railway at Craven Arms and the 1849 Shrewsbury & Birmingham Railway at Wellington. It crossed the 1862 Severn Valley Railway (Shrewsbury to Hartlebury) at Buildwas. The first mentioned became known as the North & West Route and was operated by the Great Western and London & North Western Railways jointly from 1870. The second had been under the same joint control from 1854 and the third became part of the GWR in 1872.

Under an Act of 21st July 1859, the Much Wenlock & Severn Junction Railway was built over a distance of 3½ miles. It opened on the same day as the SVR, 1st February 1862, branching from it at Buildwas.

The Wellington & Severn Junction Railway was built under an Act of 28th August 1853 and was opened south to Horsehay for freight on 1st May 1857. It was extended to Lightmoor in 1858 and opened to passengers between Wellington and Coalbrookdale on 2nd May 1859. The service continued to Shifnal by reversing onto the S&BR Madeley branch, which had opened for goods back in November 1854.

The Much Wenlock, Craven Arms & Coalbrookdale Railway (usually termed the Wenlock Railway) was incorporated on 22nd July 1861 and opened between Buildwas and Coalbrookdale on 1st November 1864 and from Much Wenlock to Presthope on 5th December of that year. Services ran through to Craven Arms from 16th December 1867. GWR trains began running between Lightmoor and Coalbrookdale on 1st November 1864, where double track was provided.

The GWR took over the S&BR in 1854, the W&SJR in 1892 and the MW&SJR in 1895. The changes to the Madeley branch are listed under that heading

British Railways Western Region incorporated the GWR upon nationalisation in 1948 and all services were withdrawn between Craven Arms and Longville on 31st December 1951 and passenger trains north to Much Wenlock on the same day. They ceased to Wellington on 23rd July 1962. Freight closure between Longville and Buildwas came on 4th December 1963. The Lightmoor Junction - Ketley section closed officially on 6th July 1964, but the line from Lightmoor to Heath Hill summit remained open until May 1979 for occasional use to the crane works in Horsehay. The line through Madeley to Buildwas was still carrying coal to Ironbridge Power Station in 2008.

PASSENGER SERVICES

The initial timetable offered a 7.5am from Madeley Court to Wellington, reversing at Lightmoor, and a return journey at 10.10, this continuing through to Shifnal. There were two other similar trips each weekday, plus one on Sundays. By 1863 there were two extra trains on Monday and Thursday.

The opening of the Wenlock branch brought six weekday trains. The link between Buildwas and Lightmoor in 1864 carried a similar service, but with four Sunday trains and a simpler Madeley timetable.

With trains running from Craven Arms in 1867, there were only two through services to Wellington. The 1869 timetable showed three, with two others starting at Much Wenlock. Only these two ran on Sundays.

Madeley saw two trains on weekdays each way, running between bizarre points. This was the case to the effective end in 1915.

Much Wenlock saw similar services in 1890, but the Sunday trains were reduced to one. Short workings had increased to five by 1914, but there were no Sunday trains. World War I brought some reductions; by 1920 there were two departures from Craven Arms, with four more north from Much Wenlock. The figures were three and two in 1940 with three and three as the final figures in 1951. The last timetable, in 1962, showed seven departures from Much Wenlock, weekdays only.

A brief flicker of life was to be seen in the BR Summer timetable for 1990, when there were departures shown on Sundays from Birmingham New Street at 09.50 and 15.20 to Ironbridge Gorge and back. There had been similar, but unrecorded, services since 1979.

June 1869

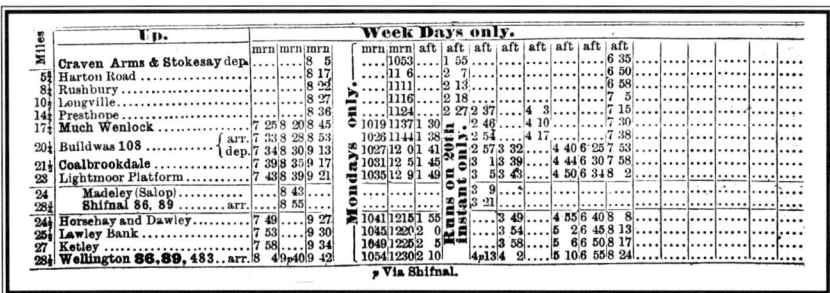

February 1890

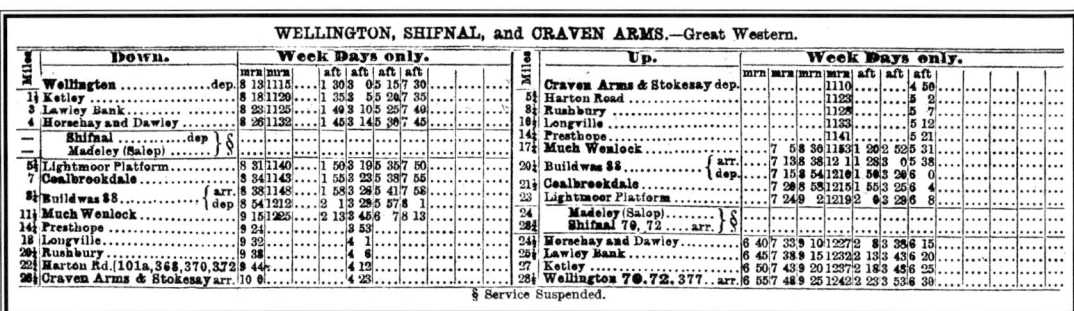

July 1914

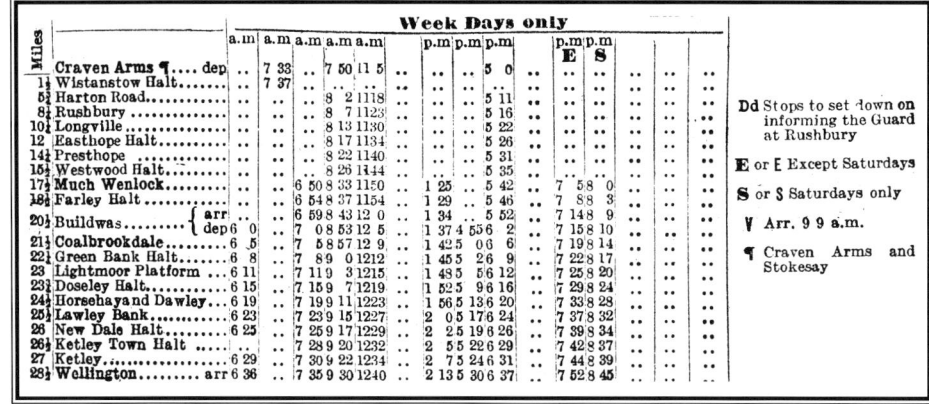

June 1920

June 1951

Table 157 WELLINGTON and MUCH WENLOCK—(Third class only)

Week Days only

Miles		am	am	am	pm S	pm	pm B	pm	pm	pm	pm S
—	**Wellington** dep	6 48	8 16	1117	..	3 10	..	4 30	5 50	7 55	10 0
1¼	Ketley	6 53	8 20	1121	1245	3 15	..	4 34	5 54	8 0	10 5
2	Ketley Town Halt	..	8 23	1123	1246	3 17	..	4 36	5 56	8 1	10 7
2½	New Dale Halt	6 57	8 25	1125	1249	3 20	..	4 39	5 58	8 4	1010
3	Lawley Bank	7 0	8 28	1128	1254	3 23	..	4 42	6 0	8 7	1013
4	Horsehay and Dawley	7 5	8 33	1133	1 0	3 28	..	4 47	6 4	8 12	1018
4½	Doseley Halt	7 8	8 36	1136	1 4	3 31	..	4 50	6 7	8 15	1021
5½	Lightmoor Platform	7 13	8 40	1140	1 10	3 35	..	4 54	6 10	8 19	1025
6¼	Green Bank Halt	7 16	8 42	1143	1 13	3 38	..	4 57	6 12	8 22	..
7	**Coalbrookdale**	7 19	8 45	1146	1 19	3 41	4 10	5 1	6 14	8 25	..
8	Buildwas arr	7 23	8 50	1151	1 26	3 45	4 14	5 5	6 18	8 30	..
	Buildwas dep	7 40	8 56	1155	1 35	3 46	4 15	5 6	6 20	8 31	..
10½	Farley Halt	7 50	9 3	12 4	1 43	3 54	4 24	5 14	6 29	8 39	..
11¼	**Much Wenlock** arr	7 57	9 10	1210	1 50	4 0	4 30	5 20	6 34	8 45	..

Week Days only

Miles		am	am	am	am	pm	pm B	pm	pm	pm E	pm S
—	**Much Wenlock** dep	..	6 50	8 35	1140	1 0	..	4 40	5 45	7 5	8 0
1	Farley Halt	..	6 54	8 38	1144	1 3	..	4 44	5 48	7 8	8 3
3¼	Buildwas arr	..	6 59	8 44	1150	1 9	..	4 50	5 54	7 14	8 9
	Buildwas dep	6 0	7 0	8 56	1155	1 12	3 25	4 55	6 2	7 15	8 10
4½	**Coalbrookdale**	6 5	7 5	8 59	1158	1 17	3 30	5 0	6 6	7 19	8 14
5	Green Bank Halt	6 8	7 8	9 2	12 1	1 20	3 32	5 2	6 9	7 22	8 17
5¾	Lightmoor Platform	6 11	7 11	9 5	12 5	1 23	3 35	5 5	6 12	7 25	8 20
6¾	Doseley Halt	6 15	7 15	9 10	12 9	1 27	..	5 9	6 16	7 29	8 24
7¼	Horsehay and Dawley	6 19	7 19	9 13	1213	1 31	..	5 13	6 20	7 33	8 28
8¼	Lawley Bank	6 23	7 23	9 16	1217	1 35	..	5 17	6 24	7 37	8 32
8¾	New Dale Halt	6 25	7 25	9 19	1219	1 37	..	5 19	6 26	7 39	8 34
9¼	Ketley Town Halt	..	7 28	9 22	1221	1 40	..	5 22	6 29	7 42	8 37
9¾	Ketley	6 29	7 30	9 25	1223	1 42	..	5 24	6 31	7 44	8 39
11¼	**Wellington** arr	6 36	7 35	9 34	1228	1 48	..	5 32	6 37	7 52	8 45

B Except Saturdays and School Holidays **E** Except Saturdays **S** Saturdays only

June 1955

WELLINGTON and MUCH WENLOCK

WEEK DAYS ONLY—(Second class only)

Mls		am	am	am E	am S	pm	pm	pm
—	**Wellington** dep	6 50	8 16	1117	1117	3 5	4 40	5 50
1¼	Ketley	6 56	8 21	1122	1122	3 10	4 45	5 54
2	Ketley Town Halt	..	8 23	1124	1124	3 12	4 47	5 56
2½	New Dale Halt	7 0	8 26	1126	1126	3 15	4 50	5 58
3	Lawley Bank	7 3	8 29	1129	1129	3 18	4 53	6 0
4	Horsehay and Dawley	7 8	8 34	1134	1134	3 23	4 58	6 4
4½	Doseley Halt	7 11	8 37	1137	1137	3 26	5 1	6 7
5½	Lightmoor Halt	7 14	8 40	1141	1141	3 30	5 5	6 13
6¼	Green Bank Halt	7 17	8 43	1144	1144	3 33	5 8	6 15
7	Coalbrookdale Halt	7 20	8 46	1147	1147	3 36	5 12	6 17
8	**Buildwas** arr	7 24	8 50	1151	1151	3 40	5 16	6 21
	Buildwas dep	7 28	8 52	1155	12 5	3 41	5 17	6 23
10½	Farley Halt	7 37	9 1	12 4	1214	3 50	5 26	6 32
11¼	**Much Wenlock** arr	7 42	9 6	12 9	1219	3 55	5 31	6 37

Mls		am	am	am	pm	pm	pm	pm
	Much Wenlock dep	6 50	8 30	1140	1 0	4 40	5 45	7 5
1	Farley Halt	6 54	8 34	1145	1 4	4 45	5 49	7 9
3¼	**Buildwas** arr	6 59	8 39	1150	1 9	4 50	5 54	7 14
	Buildwas dep	7 0	8 41	1155	1 11	4 55	6 2	7 15
4½	Coalbrookdale Halt	7 5	8 45	1159	1 16	5 0	6 7	7 20
5	Green Bank Halt	7 8	8 48	12 2	1 19	5 3	6 10	7 23
5¾	Lightmoor Halt	7 11	8 51	12 6	1 22	5 6	6 13	7 26
6½	Doseley Halt	7 16	8 55	1210	1 26	5 10	6 17	7 30
7¼	Horsehay and Dawley	7 20	8 59	1214	1 30	5 14	6 21	7 34
8¼	Lawley Bank	7 24	9 3	1218	1 34	5 18	6 25	7 38
8¾	New Dale Halt	7 26	9 5	1220	1 36	5 20	6 27	7 40
9¼	Ketley Town Halt	7 29	9 8	1222	1 39	5 23	6 30	7 43
9¾	Ketley	7 31	9 10	1224	1 41	5 25	6 32	7 45
11¼	**Wellington** arr	7 36	9 15	1229	1 47	5 36	6 37	7 50

E Except Saturdays. **S** Saturdays only.

September 1961

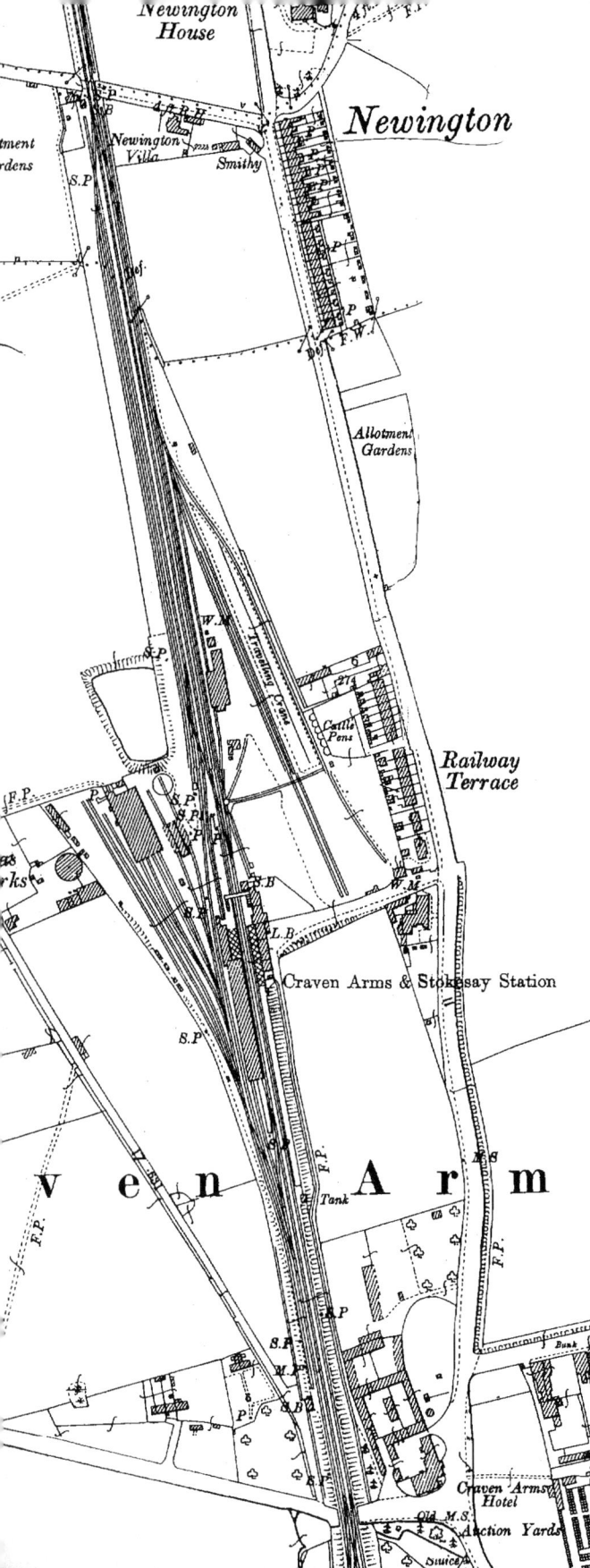

CRAVEN ARMS

II. The 1903 survey at 20ins to 1 mile has the LNWR engine shed to the right of the gasworks and the junction for the Central Wales line at the bottom. Its signal box (S.B.) was in use until 1965, when the box at the top of the map took over its work. It was then renamed simply "Craven Arms", the word "Crossing" being dropped.

↗ 1. A steam railmotor hauling two coaches is bound for the Much Wenlock route. Its number is 74 and it was in traffic from April 1906 until June 1928. (R.S.Carpenter coll.)

→ 2. No. 9630 is waiting to depart for the Much Wenlock line on 9th April 1946. Craven Arms had a staff of 42 to 46 in the 1930s and was the terminal point for trains from the Bishops Castle Railway until its closure in 1935. (E.Johnson)

→ 3. The choice of branch destinations is worthy of study in this view from about 1950. The 2-6-2T has probably just arrived from Wellington and is about to run round its two coaches. The branch trains often moved to the nearby bay to wait. (SLS coll.)

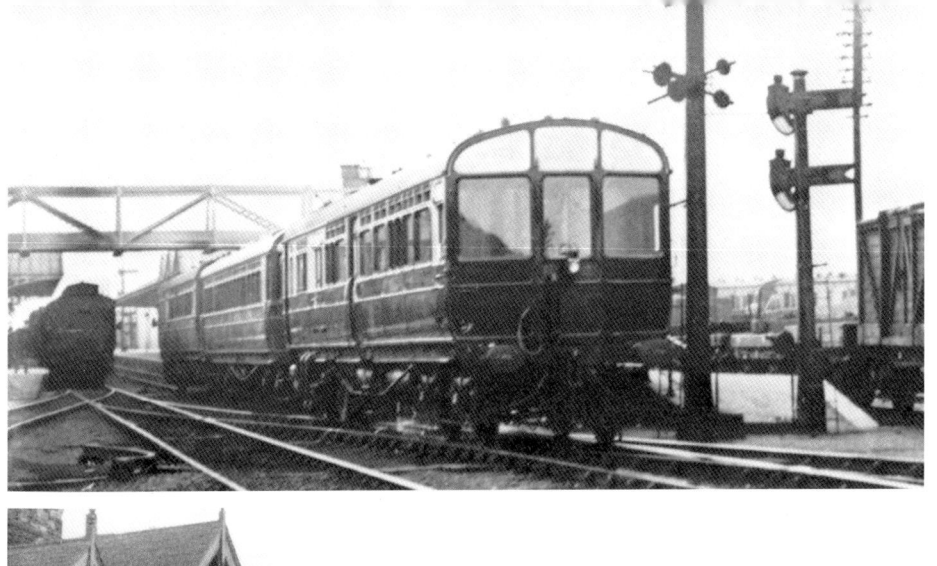

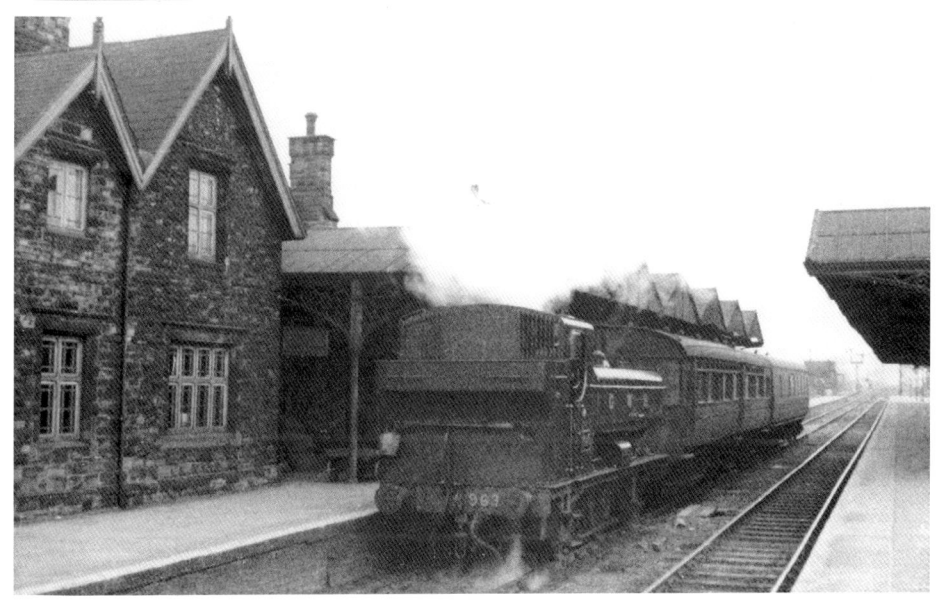

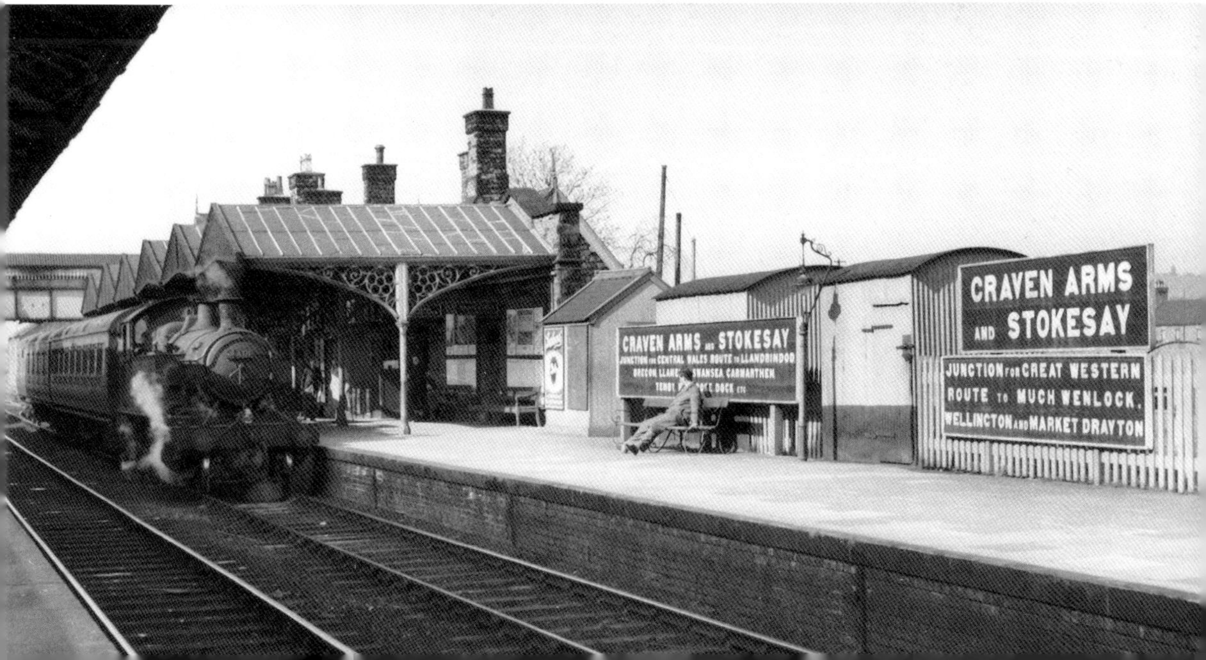
CRAVEN ARMS AND STOKESAY
JUNCTION FOR CENTRAL WALES ROUTE TO LLANDRINDOD
SWANSEA CARMARTHEN
DOCK ETC
CRAVEN ARMS AND STOKESAY
JUNCTION FOR GREAT WESTERN ROUTE TO MUCH WENLOCK, WELLINGTON AND MARKET DRAYTON

4.   Two photographs from August 1951 reveal the generous facilities provided. Looking south, Junction Box is in the distance and on the right is the bay platform at which most trains from the Central Wales line terminated. (R.G.Nelson/T.Walsh)

5.   The view north includes the six-road carriage shed, left of centre but not on the map. Also visible is the goods shed; all goods traffic ceased on 6th May 1968. (R.G.Nelson/T.Walsh)

6. An undated view includes 2-6-2T no. 4401 ready to leave for Wellington. The fine vaulted canopy and all the buildings were destroyed; a housing estate now occupies former railway land west of the main line and it has direct access to the station. The platforms were provided with bus shelters. (P.Q.Treloar coll.)

**Further views appear in *Craven Arms to Llandeilo*
and *Shrewsbury to Ludlow*.**

7. The suffix "Stokesay" was applied from July 1879 to May 1974. Stokesay Castle was the seat of Lord Craven and his coat of arms gives rise to the name of the nearby inn. The east elevation is seen in August 1965. (J.C.Gillham)

WISTANSTOW HALT

8. The halt was in use from 7th May 1934 until 11th June 1956 and was a little over one mile from Craven Arms. The village was nearby on the west side of the line. There was a small 10-lever intermediate signal box here in 1901-33. (Lens of Sutton coll.)

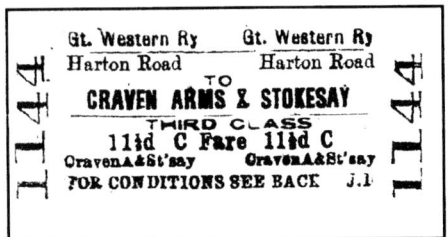 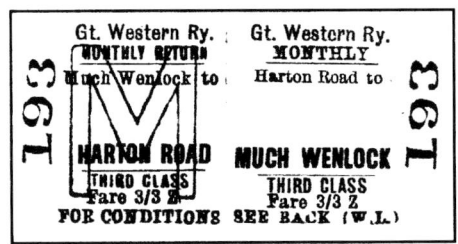

NORTH OF WISTANSTOW HALT

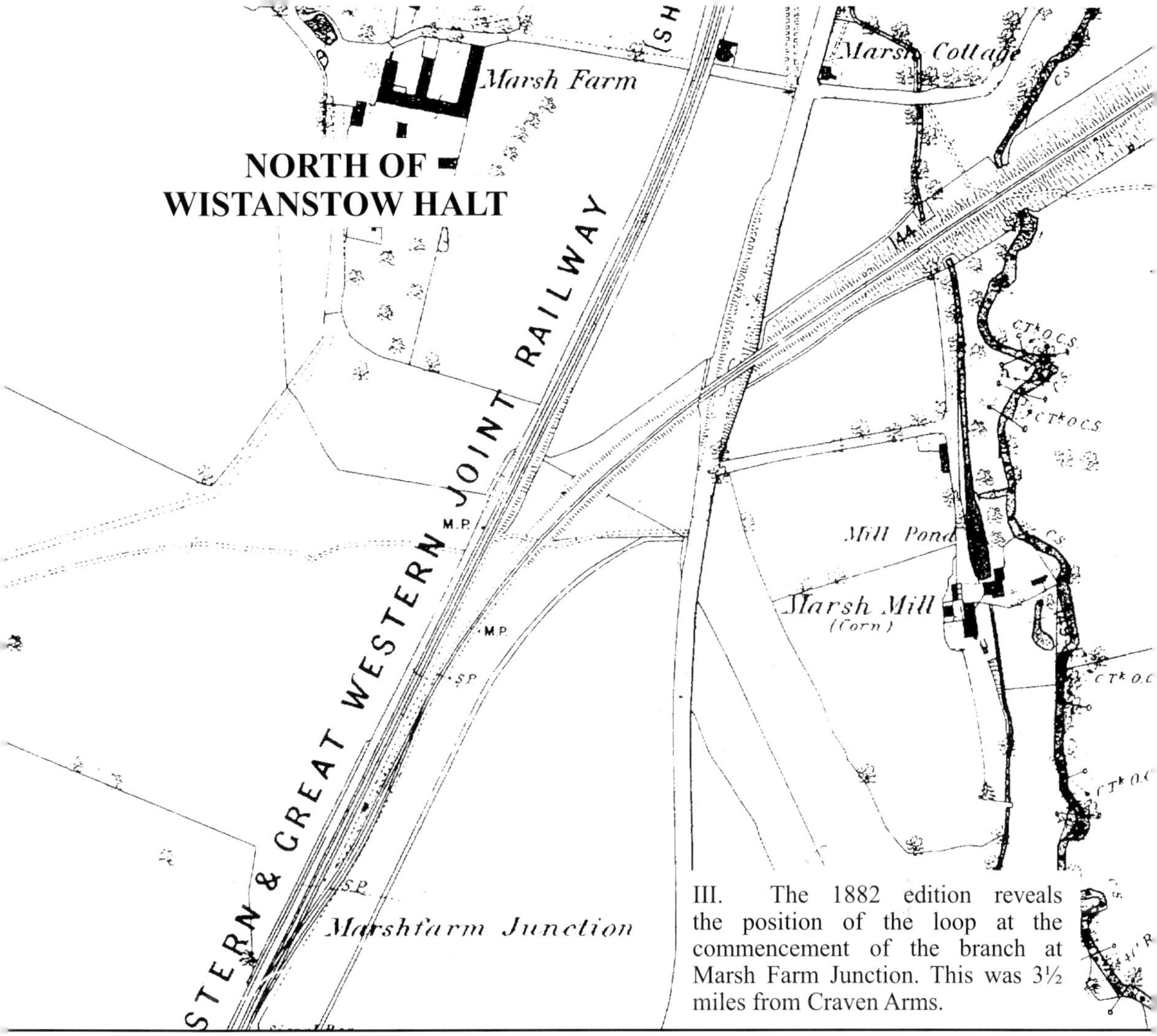

III. The 1882 edition reveals the position of the loop at the commencement of the branch at Marsh Farm Junction. This was 3½ miles from Craven Arms.

9. A view south on 27th December 1951 includes the 36-lever signal box, which was in use from September 1903 until May 1972. No. 4401 has just run onto the branch, which had only days of life left. The light engine on the right is waiting for the local train to clear the section and will continue south, tender first. (Dr L.N.Owen/R.S.Carpenter)

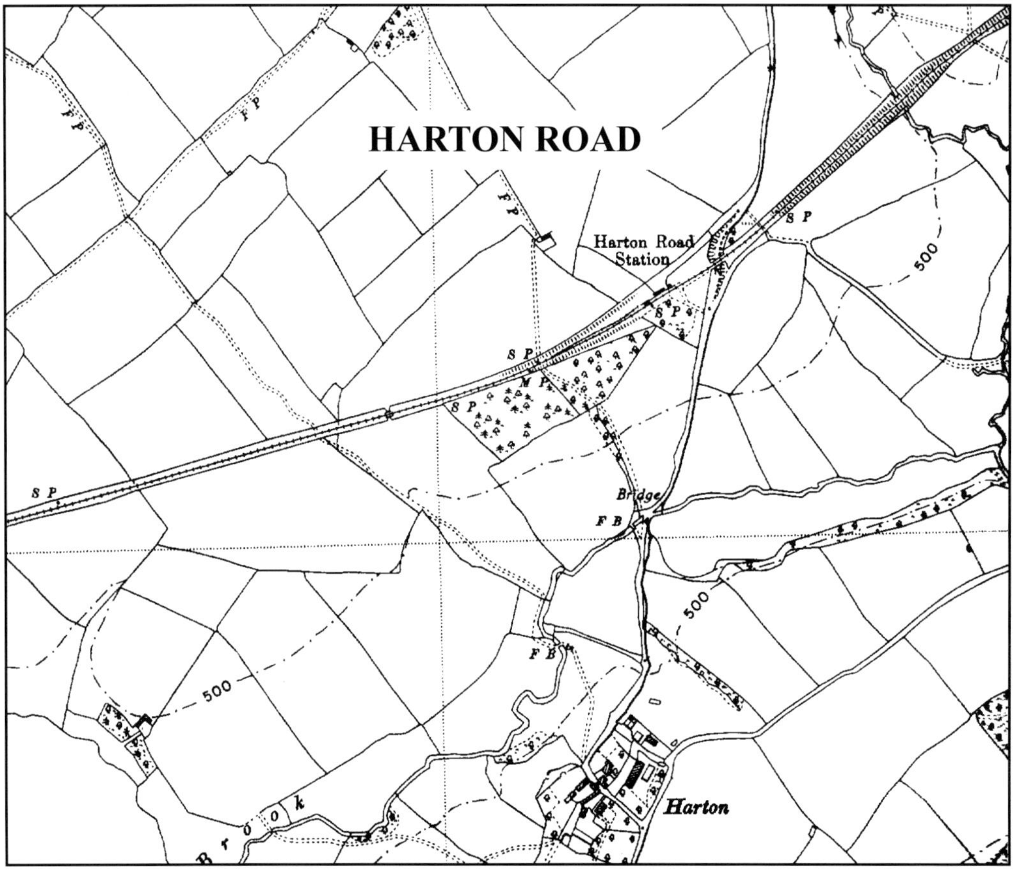

HARTON ROAD

IV. Byne Brook runs across this 1952 extract at 6ins to 1 mile.

10. This westward view from about 1930 includes the 1904 East ground frame. Until that time, there had been a signal box near the far end of the platform. (Mowat coll./Brunel University)

11. One lamp and the name board were still in place more than two years after closure. The suffix "Road" had been added in July 1881. (T.J.Edgington)

12. In the distance is part of the goods loop; this could hold seven wagons. The date is 1953 and nature was beginning to take over. (P.J.Garland/R.S.Carpenter)

13. The ground frame was still usable in September 1953 as the closed line was used for wagon storage. The distance for this activity was reduced to ½ mile in December 1955.
(P.J.Garland/
R.S.Carpenter)

14. It is now May 1961 and the site has lost its railway ambiance, but the polychromatic brickwork is still evident.
(R.G.Nelson/T.Walsh)

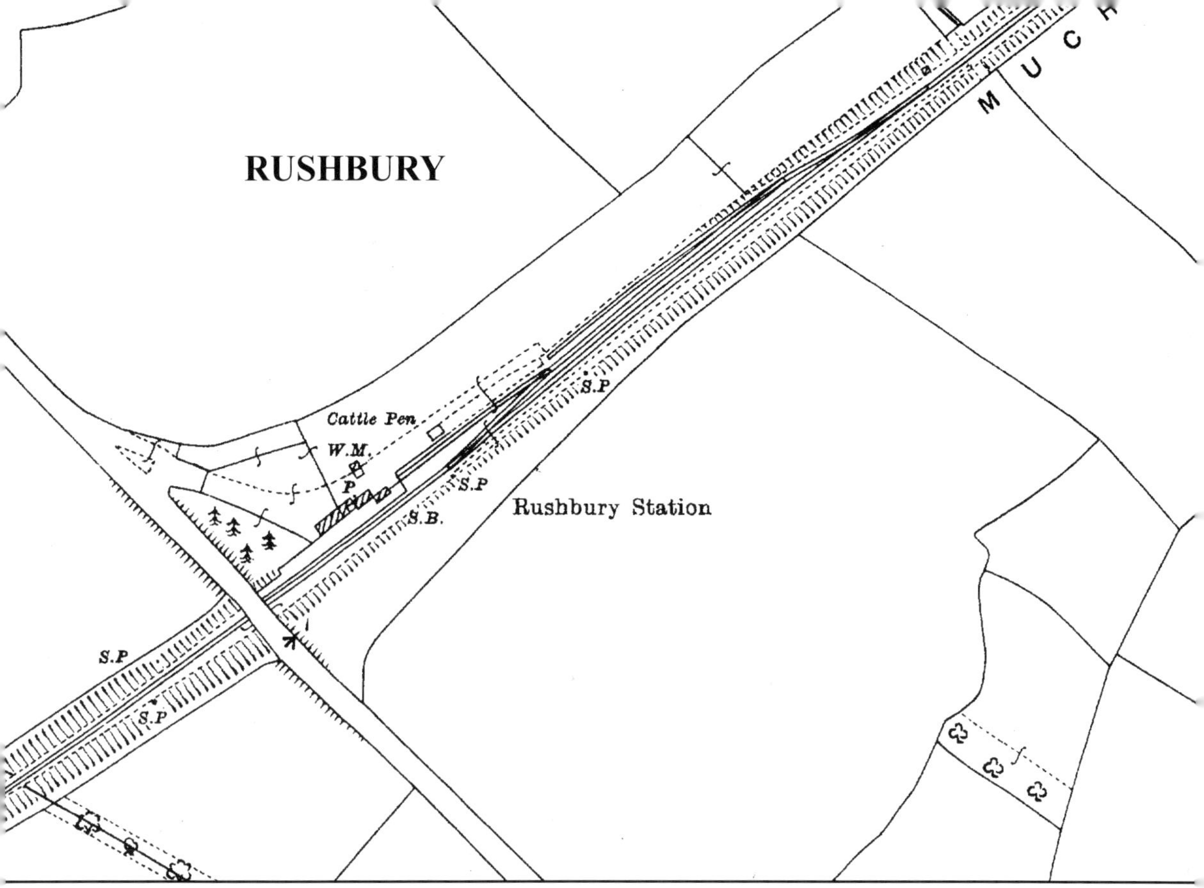

RUSHBURY

V. The 1927 survey notes that there was a weighing machine here (W.M.). The population was 572 in 1901 and the village centre was less than ½ mile distant. The northern siding had been added by 1902.

15. There was normally a staff of two here, a station master and a signalman, but they had to perform all functions between them. (Lens of Sutton coll.)

16. The signal box opened in about 1892 and lasted to the end. It had 15 levers, but was not involved in passing trains. The photograph is from 1932. (R.S.Carpenter coll.)

17. August 1952 and a Wickham trolley indicates that there was a degree of care of the closed line, if only fence maintenance. The water tank appears in no other view of ours. (R.S.Carpenter coll.)

18. It is now almost two years after closure and even the seat remains in place. Wenlock Edge is in the background, with Ape Vale below it. (P.J.Garland/R.S.Carpenter)

19. Little had changed by the time this photograph was taken in April 1962, more than ten years after closure. (J.Langford)

LONGVILLE

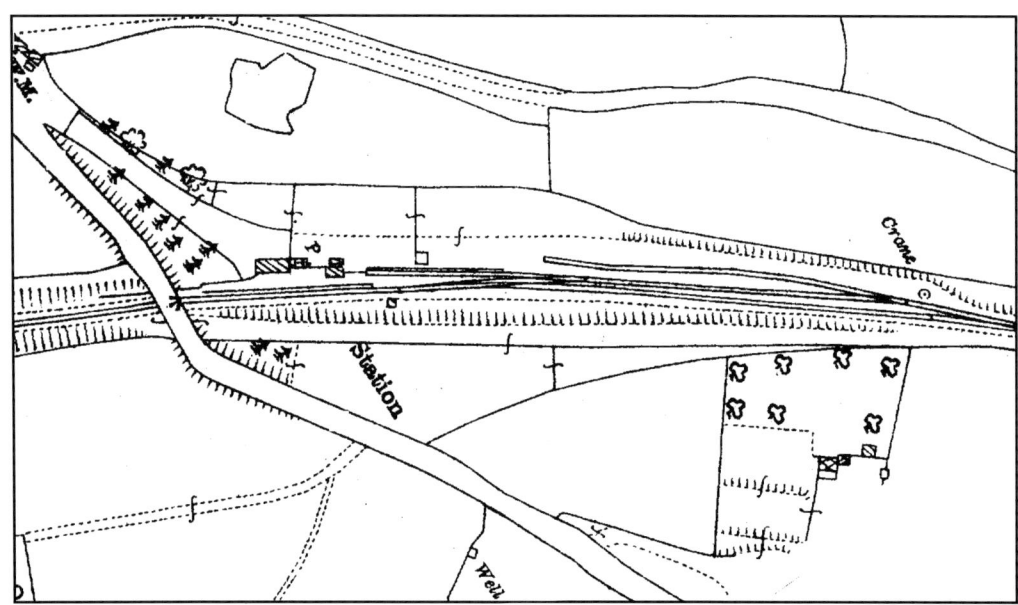

VI. The 1926 survey reveals another isolated station with a similar layout to that at Rushbury, but the upper siding was added in 1923.

20. A 1932 panorama indicates the nature of much local revenue; a variety of other local produce was also conveyed. The parcels shed at the far end of the platform had been created on the site of the signal box. (R.S.Carpenter coll.)

21. The 3.10pm from Wellington was worked by 2-6-2T no. 4401 on 21st April 1951. The line southwards would close completely at the end of that year. (W.A.Camwell/SLS)

22. A railtour made a brief visit on 12th September 1959. DMUs were never used regularly south of Much Wenlock, although a GWR unit was tried in the 1930s. (G.Adams/M.J.Stretton coll.)

23. The end of the operating line is seen on 18th May 1961, but the station building is obscured by the parcels shed. The line climbed from Craven Arms to almost 650ft above sea level here. (R.G.Nelson/T.Walsh)

24. Turning round on the same day, we note that the ground frame had given way to a single lever. This took place in October 1954. Until that time, an empty passenger train appeared each weekday acting as a parcels train. It was the 3.10pm from Wellington. (R.G.Nelson/T.Walsh)

25. This view is from 20th April 1962; total closure came at the end of the following year and other ways of getting mushrooms to market were found. This was an important crop in the area. (J.Langford)

26. Two photographs from May 2001 are included to record the remains of the station, which is a little to the east of the village of Longville in the Dale. The road sign refers to the bends on the bridge. (B.W.L.Brooksbank)

27. This is the view north from the bridge. The chimney locates the original part of the building, as seen from the same angle in picture no. 20. (B.W.L.Brooksbank)

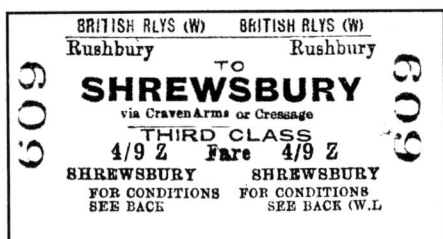

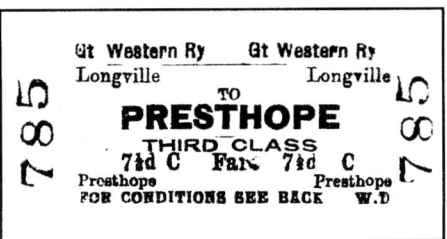

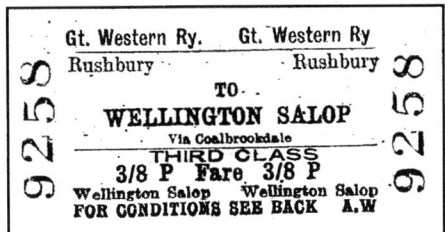

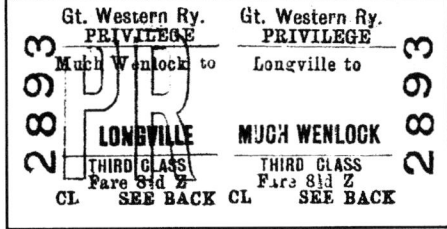

EASTHOPE HALT

28. The halt was 1½ miles from Longville and was on the east side of the line, as was the village. The route is in a linear coppice. The halt opened on 4th April 1936 and is seen in 1962 after 11 years of disuse. (J.Langford)

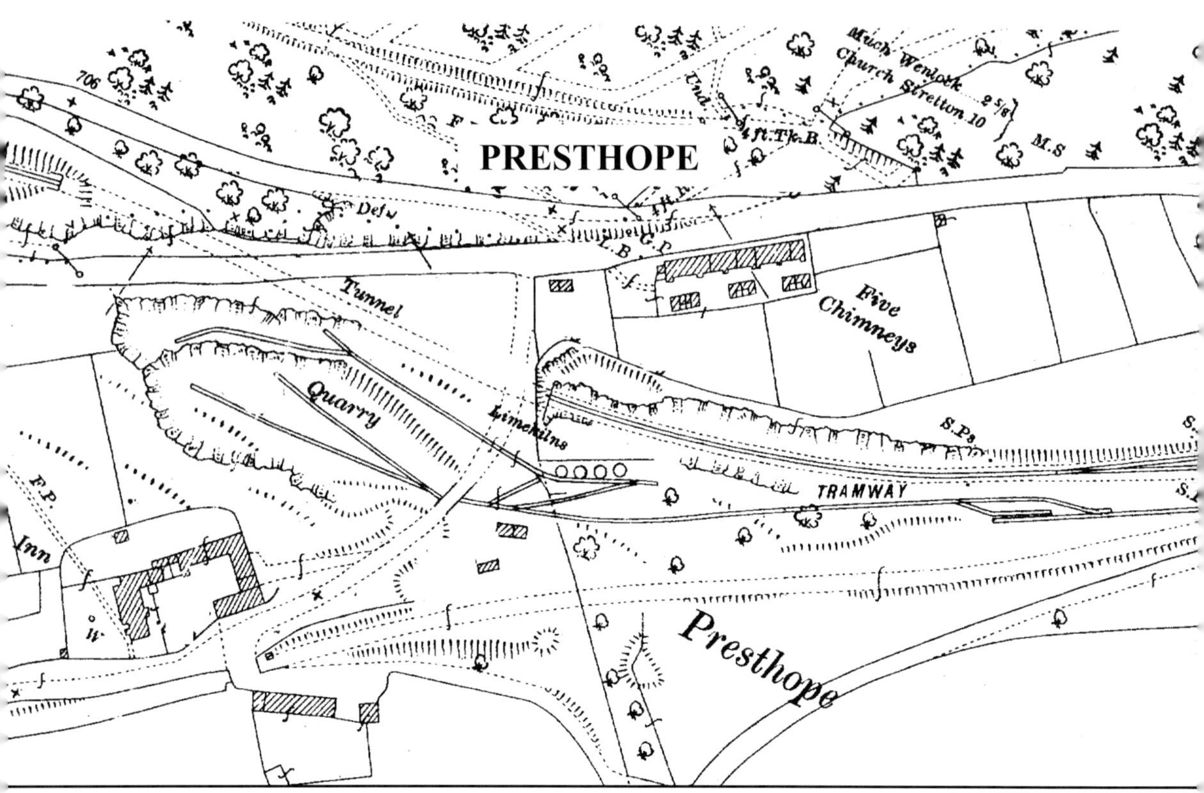

29. A southward view from 1932 has the bridge over the original quarry line on the left. It had come into use in 1867. (R.M.Casserley coll.)

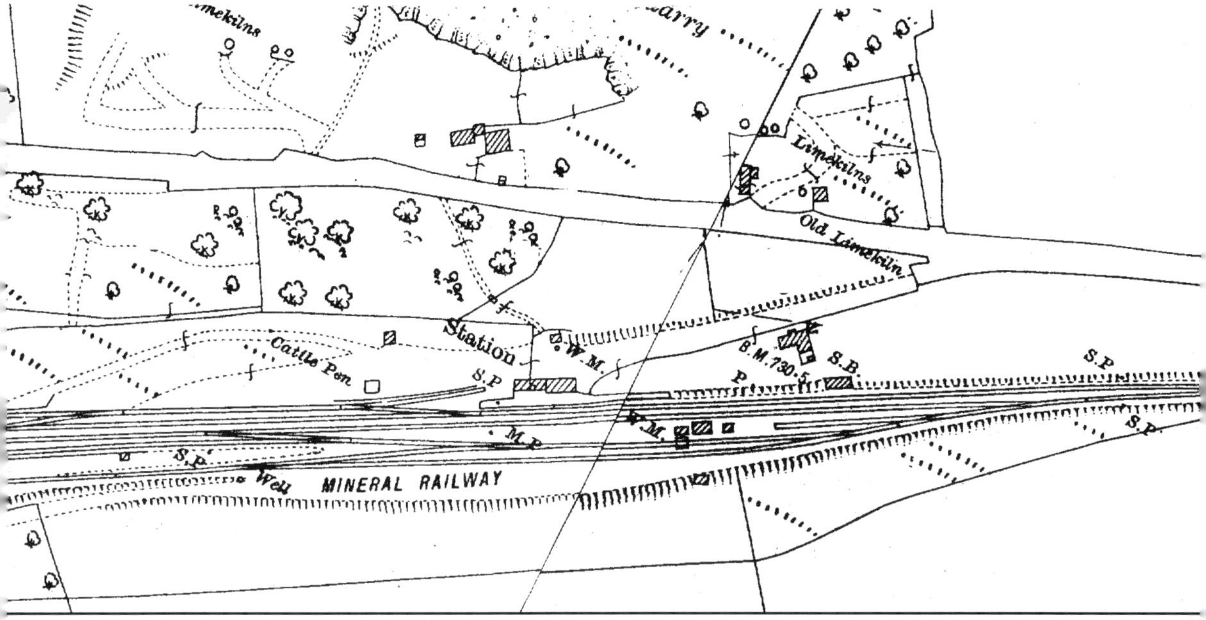

VII. The 1926 survey has the 207yd long Presthope Tunnel on the left; it was around 750ft above sea level. Below it is Knowle Limeworks, the siding to which opened on 2nd June 1926. The transfer wharf is to the left of the page break. Before that time, a longer siding, 1½ miles in length, extended between the dotted lines, under a road bridge, to a limeworks at Lilleshall Quarries.

30. The signalling remained functional for almost three years after passenger services ceased. The view is from September 1953 and includes the cattle pens. The yard could accommodate 135 wagons. (P.J.Garland/ R.S.Carpenter coll.)

31. The SLS railtour of 23rd April 1955 paused for photography, which included the unusual inside keyed track. There were other examples at Hampton Loade and on the Blagdon branch. Horsehay Yard still had some in 2008. The sidings were removed in 1960. No. 2516 was a "Dean Goods" 0-6-0. (T.J.Edgington)

32. Seen in April 1962, the signal box had a frame containing 31 levers, which were in use from 1893 until 17th October 1954. The map shows weighing machines for wagons and road vehicles. One mile distant was Westwood Siding. It served Westwood Quarry from 1886 until 1957. Westwood Halt was nearby. (J.Langford)

WESTWOOD HALT

33. The halt opened on 7th December 1935 and is seen during the freight-only period, after the shelter had gone. The level crossing on a lane to a farm is in the distance. (A.Dudman)

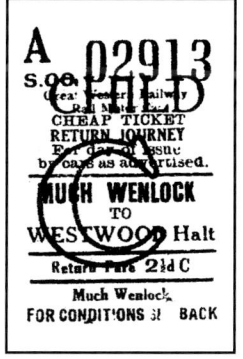
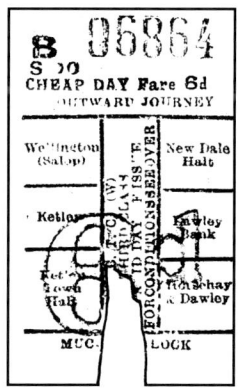

MUCH WENLOCK

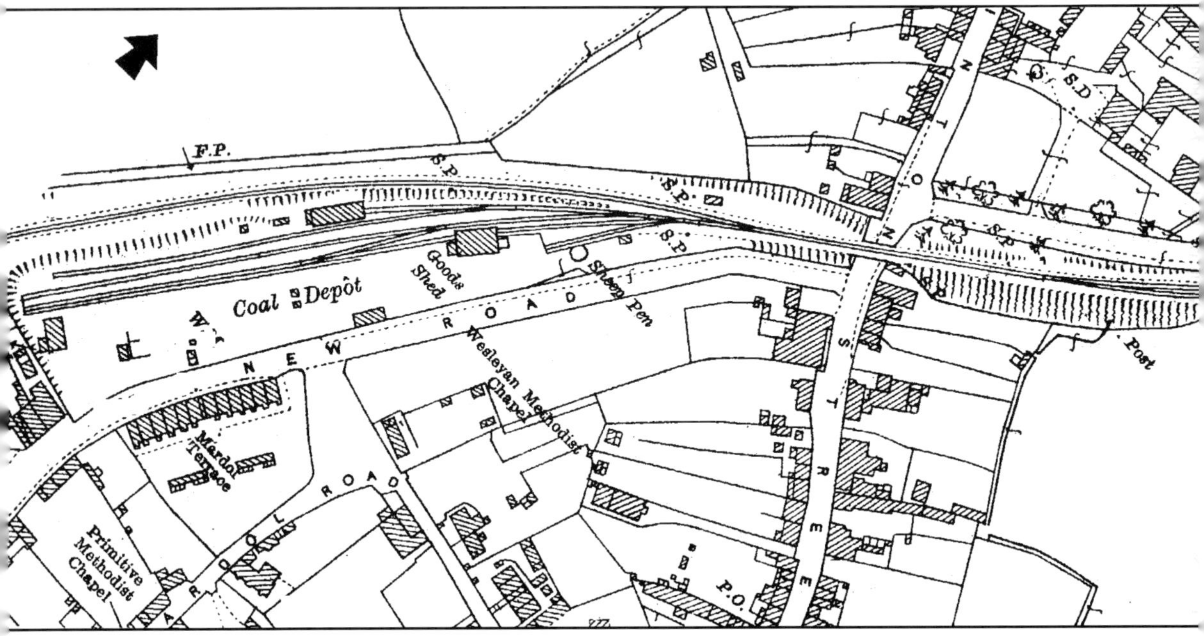

34. Two postcard views from the Edwardian era reveal the Gothic styling, despite the ivy. The signal box is from 1893. (Lens of Sutton coll.)

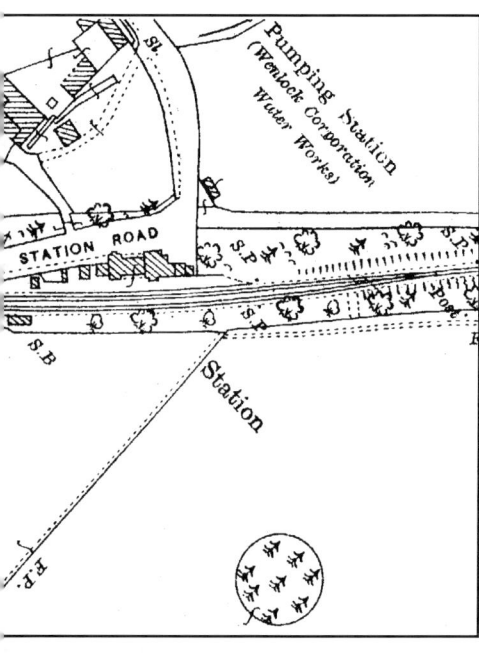

VIII. The 1926 survey has the site of the first station on the left. This terminus site was devoted to coal and goods when the through station (right) opened on 16th December 1867.

35. On the left is the parcels shed and in the distance is the Linden Walk footbridge. The loop was for goods trains only. The staff usually numbered 12 in the 1930s. (Lens of Sutton coll.)

36. Seen in 1932, the goods yard had an exceptionally long dock due to it having been built for passenger trains. The longest siding could accommodate 58 wagons.
(Mowat coll./Brunel University)

37. The engine shed could house two locomotives and was in use until the end of 1951. Water came from a reservoir further up the valley. The photograph is from 1949. (R.S.Carpenter coll.)

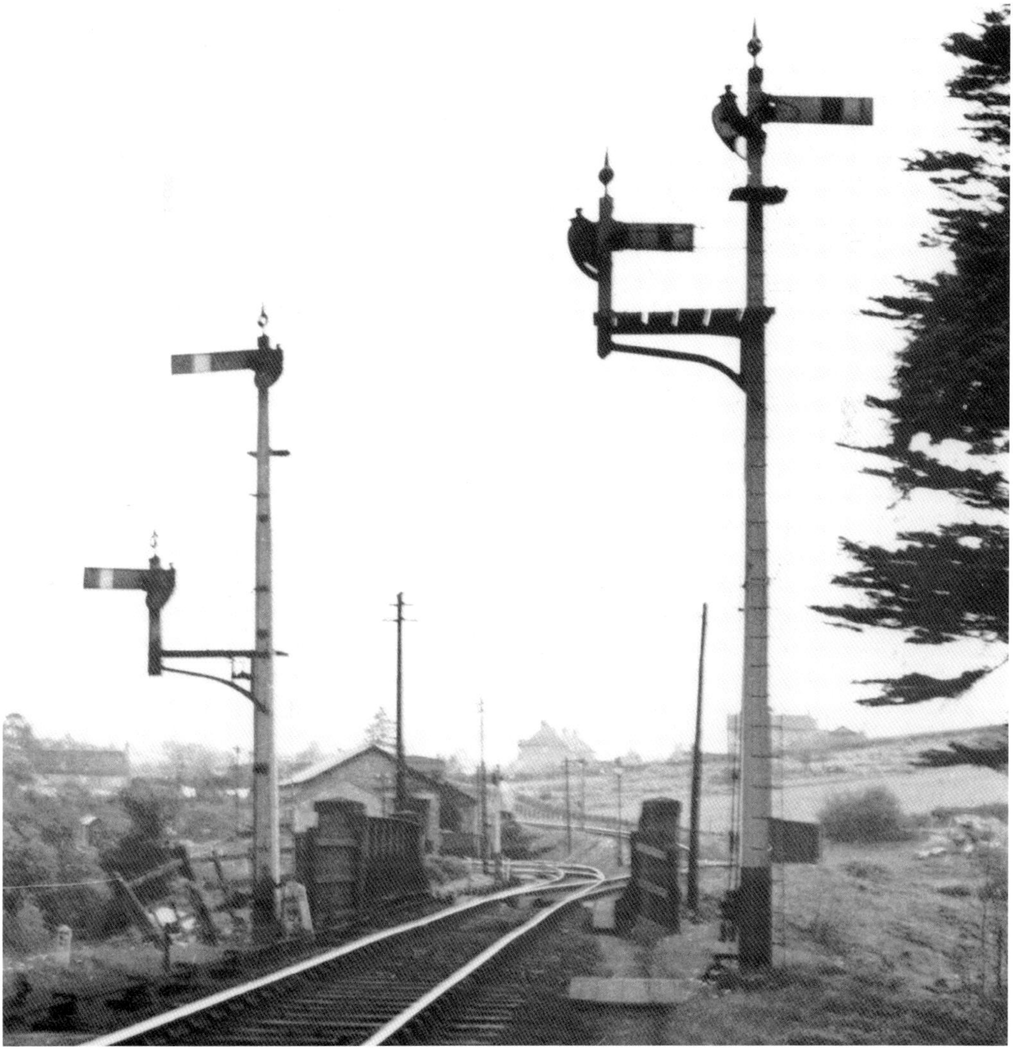

38. Another 1949 view: from left to right the signals are for the goods yard, Presthope, the loop and the platform. The goods shed is partially obscured by the parapet of the road bridge. (J.Moss/R.S.Carpenter coll.)

133 BRITISH RLYS (W) BRITISH RLYS (W) 133
Presthope Presthope
TO
WOLVERHAMPTON
ViaCoalb'dale & Well'Sa
THIRD CLASS
5/5 Z Fare 5/5 Z
Wolverhampton Wolverhampton
FOR CONDITIONS FOR CONDITIONS
SEE BACK SEE BACK W.D

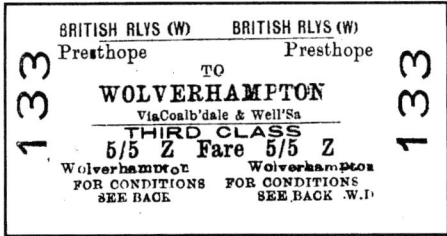

39. On the right is the 1867 WMR signal box, which was used as a guards room in later years. Its 1893 successor (opposite) had a 31-lever frame and was in use until line closure. (J.Moss/R.S.Carpenter coll.)

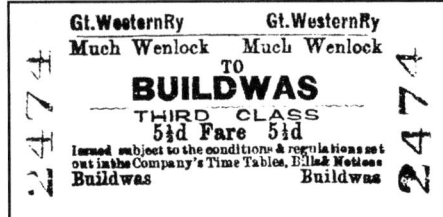

40. A visit to the goods yard reveals that a grain store was attached to the goods shed. The cattle pens are not on the map either, but it shows an unusual circular sheep pen. Ex-GWR 2-6-2T no. 4409 is near the coal wagon. (J.Moss/R.S.Carpenter coll.)

41. Turning round, we can see the catch points protecting the running line, which is behind the permanent way hut on the left. The lamp was of some age by 1949. (J.Moss/R.S.Carpenter coll.)

42. Our final 1949 view was taken from the former passenger platform. For many years, there was an 0-4-2T and an 0-6-0PT allocated here. In 1921 it was nos 557 and 1531, while in 1934 it was nos 5811 and 1779. (J.Moss/R.S.Carpenter coll.)

➔ 43. Mixed trains of this type were a common feature of the working of the route. The locomotive is no. 2718, but the date was not recorded. Adjacent to the water column is a "fire devil", a precaution against freezing. (N.R.Knight/SLS coll.)

➔ 44. The southwest elevation was recorded in 1959, along with the lamp room (right) and a Hillman 10 of 1934 vintage. The local population was 2210 in 1901 and 2351 in 1961, not a recipe for heavy traffic. (H.C.Casserley)

45. Three photographs from about 1960 extend our survey. Seen from the approach road is the accommodation for the station master, this being the two-storey part. The bay window was to enable him to keep the site under observation. (R.S.Carpenter)

➡ 46. The driver of no. 3732 stands near the water valve, as the fireman watches the level rise. The severe gradients from Wellington demanded much of his energy and also much water. (R.S.Carpenter)

➡ 47. All but the extremity of the chimney was constructed from local grey limestone. The fire was in the corner of the clerk's office and inside the shed was a 30cwt crane. Goods traffic ceased on 2nd December 1963, but the track was retained by the engineers. (R.S.Carpenter)

48. Not seen in other photographs is the weigh house - right. The picture is from about 1962, when the line in the foreground was used a few times each week and passenger trains ran as far as the station; hence the spare coach in the yard. (J.Moss/R.S.Carpenter coll.)

➜ 49. No. 4178 is departing with the 4.40pm to Wellington on 21st July 1962, the last day of passenger service. This locomotive type was introduced in 1929. (L.W.Rowe)

➜ 50. Even the superb ridge tiles were retained during the conversion to residential use. The result is seen in 2004. The Guildhall is the centrepiece amongst the architectural gems to be enjoyed in this historic town. (B.W.L.Brooksbank)

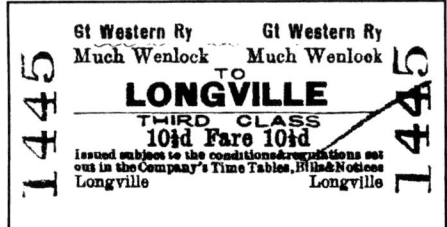

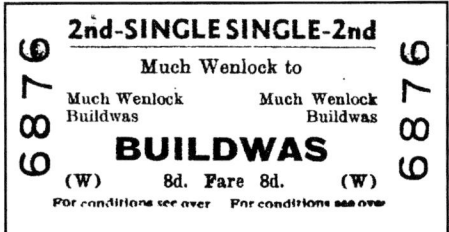

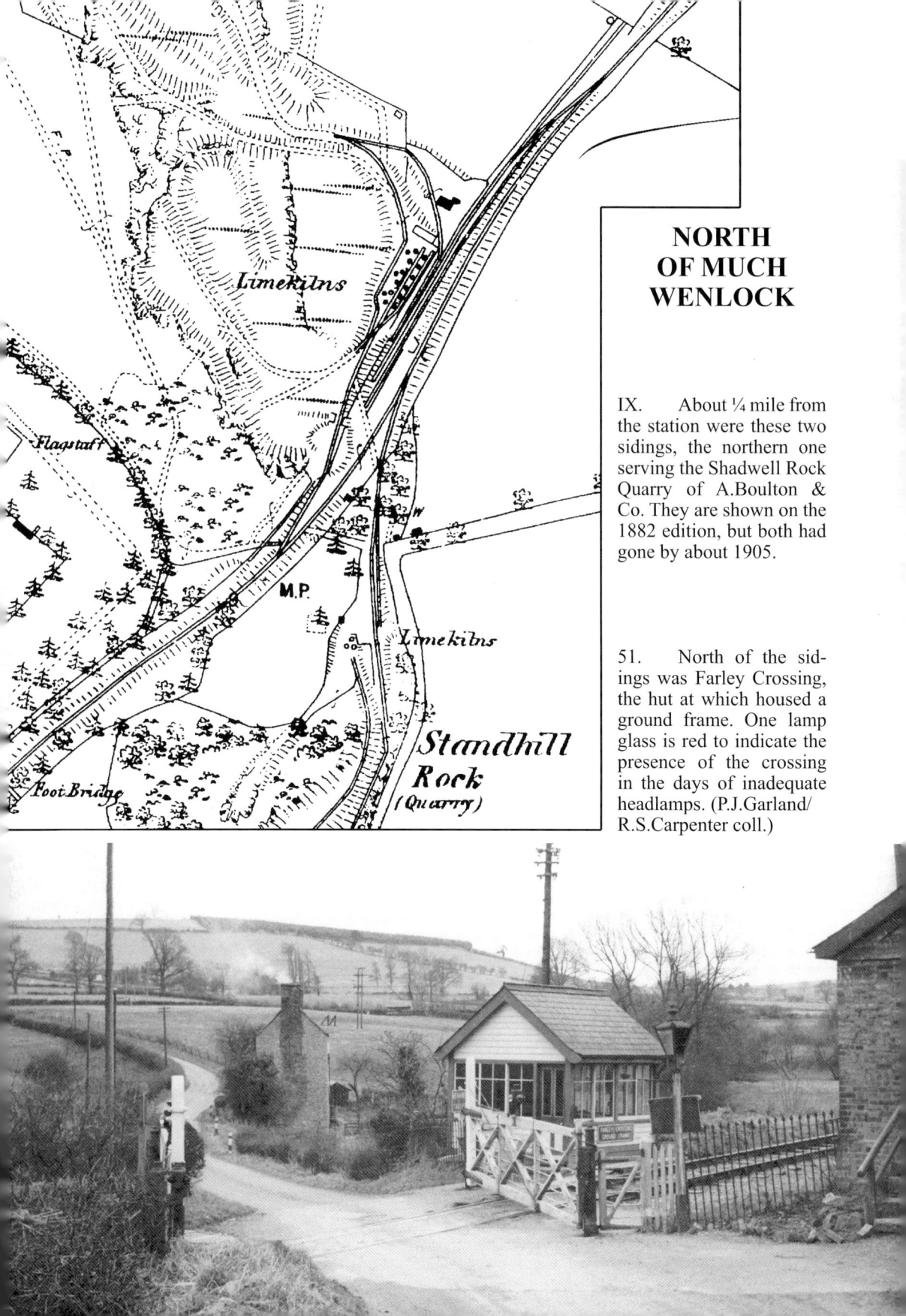

NORTH OF MUCH WENLOCK

IX. About ¼ mile from the station were these two sidings, the northern one serving the Shadwell Rock Quarry of A.Boulton & Co. They are shown on the 1882 edition, but both had gone by about 1905.

51. North of the sidings was Farley Crossing, the hut at which housed a ground frame. One lamp glass is red to indicate the presence of the crossing in the days of inadequate headlamps. (P.J.Garland/ R.S.Carpenter coll.)

FARLEY HALT

52. The halt opened on 27th October 1934 and was about ¾ mile north of Shadwell Rock Quarry. This view is towards Buildwas. (Lens of Sutton coll.)

53. Looking in the other direction, we see a siding which was first used to serve the Bradley limeworks of A.Boulton & Co. in the 1880s. The line closed in 1931 and in 1938 it reopened to serve a petrol store established on the quarry site by the Air Ministry. This closed in 1948 and was discovered full of stale petrol in 1963. Several tanker trains were run, with a class 20 diesel at each end. (Lens of Sutton coll.)

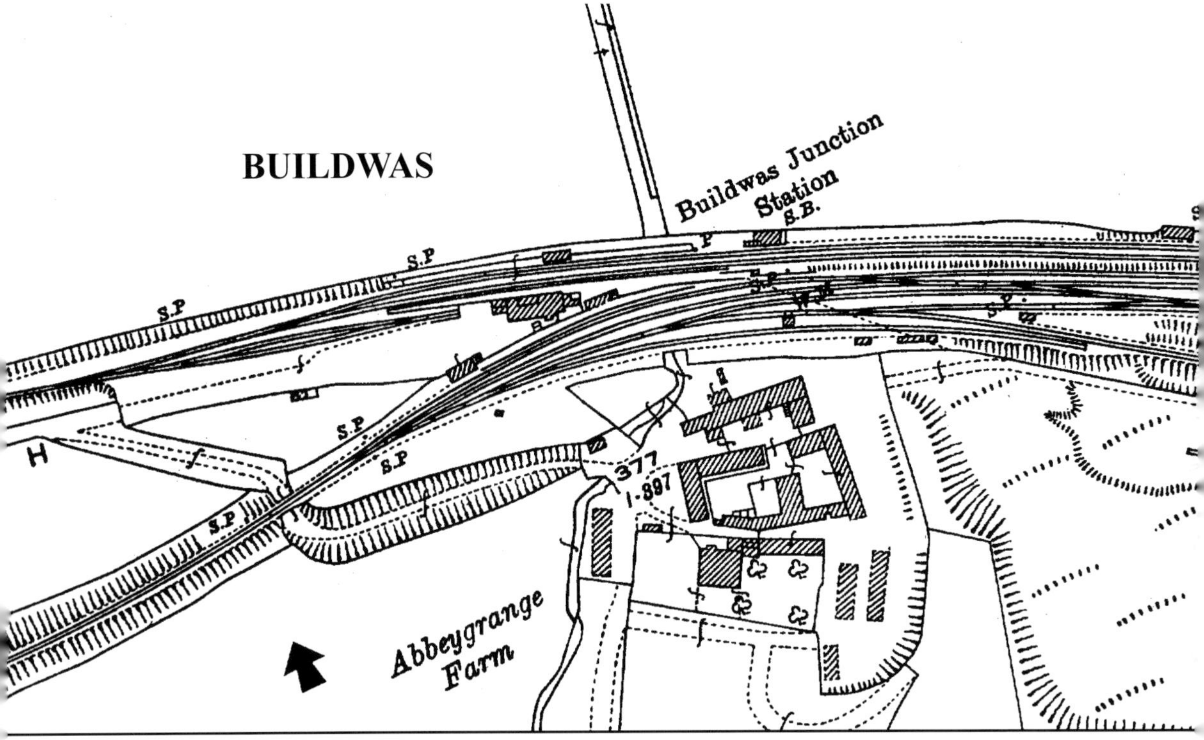

BUILDWAS

X. The 1927 edition has our route from the lower left. A siding to a pumping station on the bank of the River Severn is top right, with the Severn Valley line across the pages. The upper pair on the right run to Coalbrookdale. The station approach road is on the left.

54. It is difficult to see on the map that there were three platforms: two for Severn Valley trains and one for the Much Wenlock line. This is the latter in the 1920s, with exchange sidings on the right. (Stations UK)

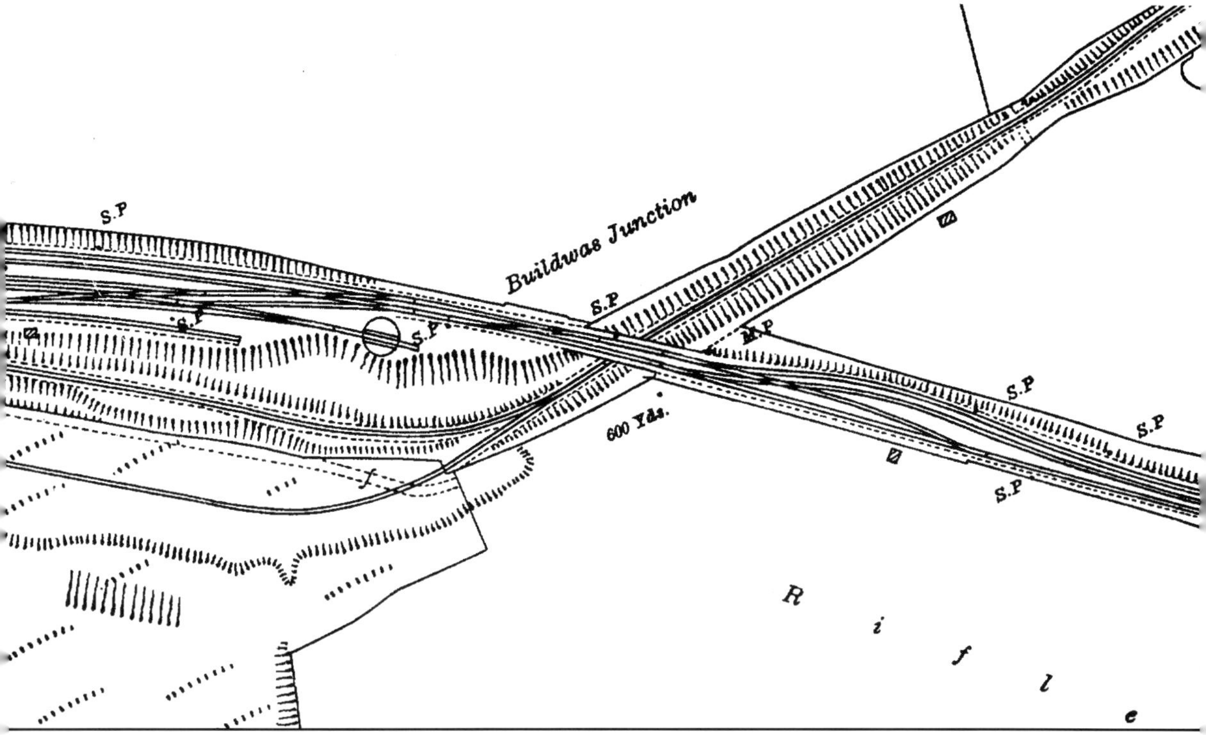

55. This is the train seen earlier in picture 31 at Presthope. In the background is the 1932 power station, which became known as Ironbridge 'A'. It had seven parallel sidings north of the platforms. (W.A.Camwell/SLS coll.)

56. The West Midlands Joint Electricity Authority became the British Electricity Authority upon nationalisation in 1948 and its initials are seen on its Peckett 0-4-0ST on 23rd April 1955. It was Ironbridge No.1. (H.F.Wheeller/R.S.Carpenter coll.)

➜ 57. Recorded on the same day was 0-6-0PT no. 4605, running in with a Wellington to Much Wenlock service. There had been a turntable at the far end of the sidings until about 1936. (H.F.Wheeller/R.S.Carpenter coll.)

➜ 58. The 11.40am Much Wenlock to Wellington was hauled by 0-6-0PT no. 9639 on 17th April 1959. The Severn Valley up platform is largely hidden by the barrow. The steps and boarded crossing linked all three platforms. (H.C.Casserley)

59. Later that day, a train starts on the stiff climb south from the station, while we examine the connections to the marshalling yard. (H.C.Casserley)

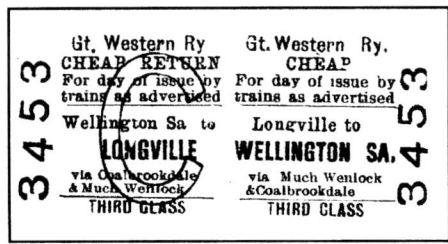

60. Nearest is no. 5167 with a Wellington to Much Wenlock service on 31st August 1959. At the far end of the platform is an 0-6-0PT with a train running in the opposite direction. (F.Hornby)

61. The station approach was used by locals, power station workers and visitors to Buildwas Abbey. It is seen on 18th May 1961, along with the siding for local goods traffic, which ceased on 2nd December 1963. (R.G.Nelson/T.Walsh)

62. No. 9639 waits with a Much Wenlock to Wellington train on 7th July 1962. Buildwas had a population of a little over 300 at that time. (P.Kingston)

> **Other views of this station can be found in our *Kidderminster to Shrewsbury* album in pictures 95-101.**

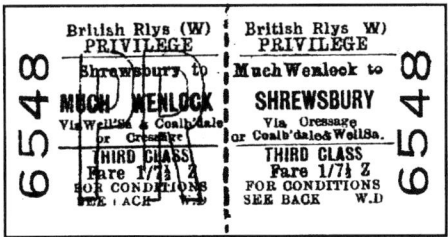

63. A DMU is bound for Wellington on 21st June 1962, as a Severn Valley train departs south. This service was withdrawn on 9th September 1963. Near the right boarder was the signal box, which had 113 levers and was in use from November 1923 until March 1964. (G.Tilt)

64. On the last day of operation, 21st July 1962, the train was lengthened and 2-6-2T no. 4178 was in charge. Ironbridge 'B' power station was built on this site and opened in 1970. (L.W.Rowe)

65. Upon privatisation, National Power took over, followed by Power Gen. EWS No. 66099 is returning to Walton Old Junction, near Warrington, with empty wagons on 18th October 2006. (E.Sharp)

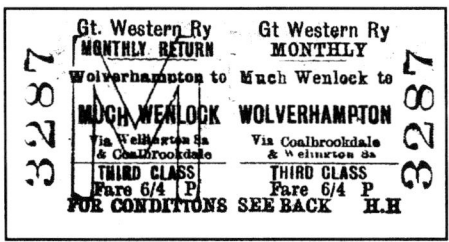

EAST OF BUILDWAS

66. The power station often consumes 2500 tons of coal per week and the line via Madeley was the one retained for its conveyance. This involves crossing the River Severn on the Albert Edward or Royal Albert Bridge. No. 47290 is doing so on 14th April 1978 and is hauling a merry-go-round train, although this principle cannot be employed at Buildwas, owing to the landform. Oil traffic began in 1976. The bridge components were cast in Coalbrookdale and the original wrought iron and timber deck was replaced in 1933 by steel beams and plates. It is a close relation to the Victoria Bridge, which is also still in use, downstream. (T.Heavyside)

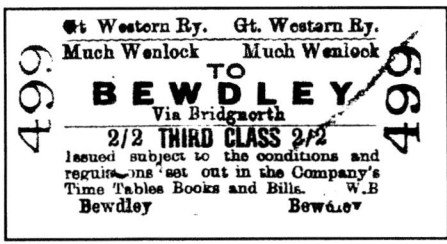

XI. The 1928 survey at 6ins to 1 mile has the Royal Albert Bridge lower left. The station is marked Sta. after the second curve and Lightmoor Junction is top right. Here, the Wellington route diverges to the top of the page and the Madeley line continues straight to the right border. Ironbridge is lower right and the area is regarded as the cradle of the industrial revolution. Careful study of the map will reveal extensive evidence of earlier industries. Some of the shafts and adits produced not only coal and iron, but oil shale as well. (Above centre is Oilhouse Coppice). A siding descends from the station northwards into the main works and from it are extensive tramways. An early extension ran to the north bank of the Severn, where local products were loaded into vessels.

67. A postcard view looking northwards in around 1900 includes the commencement of the siding to Coalbrookdale Works. On the left are the points to the two-siding goods yard, which closed on 6th July 1964. (Lens of Sutton coll.)

68. At the commencement of the siding there was a loop which facilitated transfer of traffic and the gate to the private sidings was beyond it. The photograph is from May 1961; the sidings closed on 5th July 1964. The works had built their own locomotives, six in number. (R.G.Nelson/T.Walsh)

69. The signal box had 15 levers and was in use from 1893 to 1958, after which time it functioned as a ground frame and all signals were removed. Most glass had gone by 21st June 1962. (G.Tilt)

70. A DMU bound for Much Wenlock arrives on the same day. There had been no staff here since 1st October 1956, thus the attractive yellow brick building became rather neglected. (G.Tilt)

71. Coalbrookdale Viaduct is 264yds in length and curves round the historic building which is now part of the Ironbridge Gorge Museum. It was photographed on 26th July 1987, when the double track was carrying heavy coal traffic to Ironbridge Power Station. (M.Dart)

72. No. 47196 is hauling a loaded coal train over the viaduct on 14th April 1978. A platform was opened on 27th May 1979 on the up line to serve the museum complex and three DMU trips were operated from Birmingham via Wolverhampton and a return trip over the Albert Edward bridge, on Summer Sundays. (T.Heavyside)

GREENBANK HALT

73. The platforms came into use on 12th March 1934 and were photographed on the last day of passenger trains. (G.Tilt)

74. The halt was close to the north end of the viaduct and 0-6-0PT no. 9639 has just passed over the nearby road bridge. (G.Tilt)

LIGHTMOOR PLATFORM

75. There was a station here between 2nd May 1859 and 1st November 1864, but these platforms were not provided until 12th August 1907. They were closed between 1st January 1917 and 23rd June 1919. This view is towards the junction in 1932. (Mowat coll./Brunel University)

76. Looking in the other direction, we see the commencement of the double track section, which continues to Buildwas. (Lens of Sutton coll.)

77. A June 1962 view includes the 1951 signal box, which was built on the opposite side of the track to the one shown on the map. Closer views from 1962 follow. (G.Tilt)

→ 78. The new signal box had 31 levers and replaced one built in 1875 with 25. The Madeley lines converge on the right and the Wellington ones in the distance. The box closed in 2006 when the track was singled. (G.Tilt)

→ 79. The Madeley line is on the left and the Wellington one on the right. The overgrown ones served the goods yard, which closed on 6th July 1964. We divert from our journey to visit the first route in the area, which opened in 1854. (G.Tilt)

Madeley Branch
MADELEY SALOP

XIII. Opened as Madeley on 2nd May 1859, the station was renamed Madeley Court in October 1884, and Madeley Salop on 4th June 1897. It was closed on 22nd March 1915 and reopened briefly from 13th July 1925 to 21st September of the same year, using the name shown above. The lower line on the left was a headshunt.

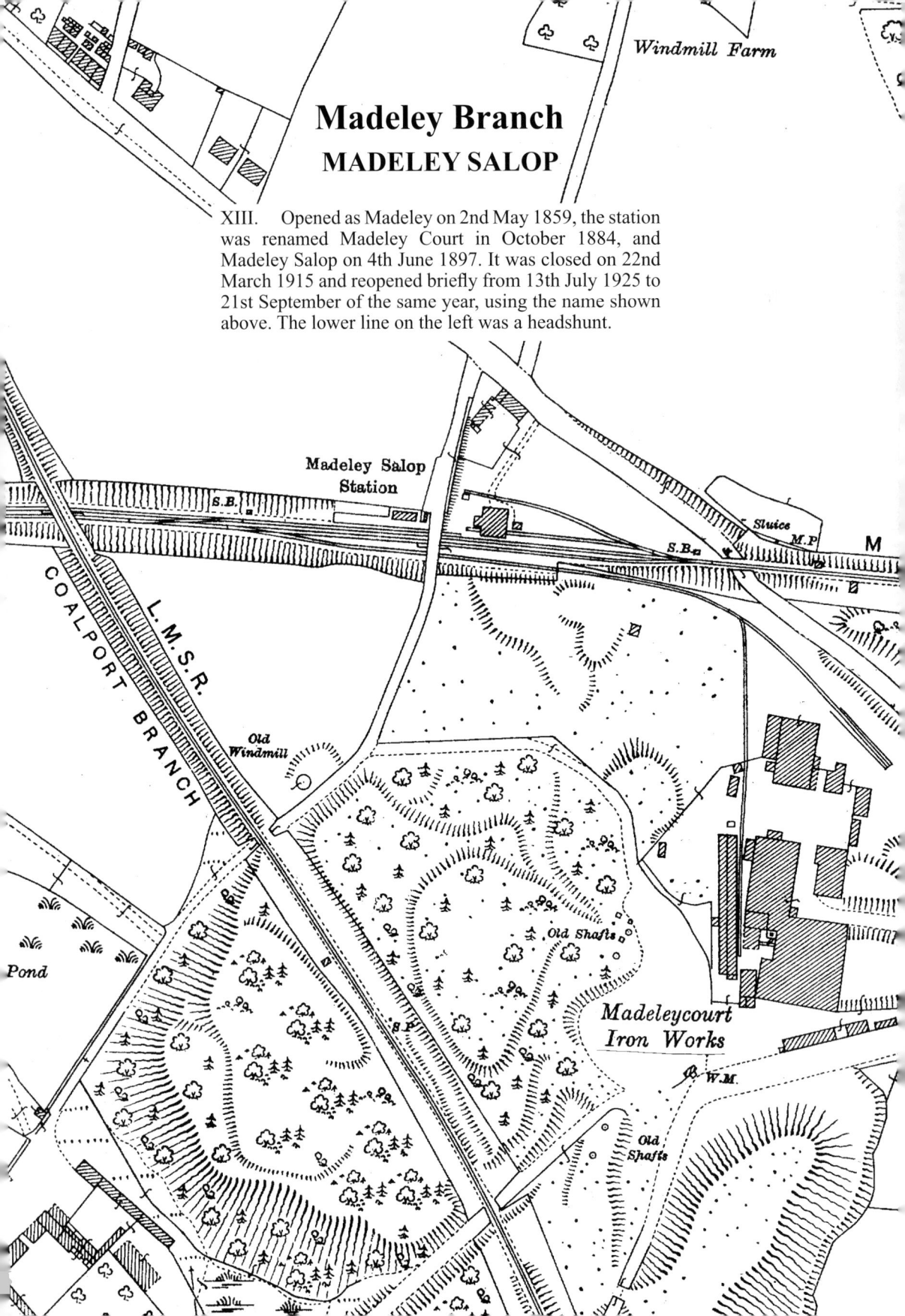

80. A postcard shows the later name on the board. Kemberton Colliery had sidings east hereof from 1870. The goods shed (centre) housed a 30cwt crane. Madeley had a population of 8100 in 1925 and the station had a staff of five. (Lens of Sutton coll.)

81. The siding on the right led to Court Works and was in use until 1964, when general goods traffic also ceased. The picture is from 1932, when the works was producing iron castings for the electrical industry. (Mowat coll./Brunel University)

NORTH OF MADELEY

82. Madeley Junction is seen on 23rd April 1955 as the SLS Special (shown in pictures 31 and 55) leaves the branch to proceed to Shifnal via a crossover. The signal box was in use from 1925 to 1969, when a new one was opened. This was still in use in 2008 controlling a long section of main line, plus the junction for coal trains. (T.J.Edgington)

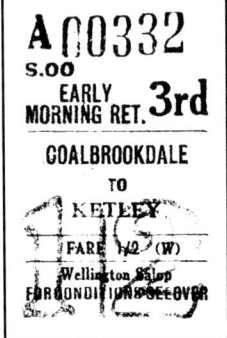 

DOSELEY HALT

83. We return to our route. Opening of this halt took place on 1st December 1932 and the communities of Dawley Magna and Dawley Parva benefitted accordingly. The southward view is from 1962. (G.Tilt)

84. Looking in the other direction, we have a close-up of the ground frame, which remained in use until 21st July 1968. The shelter went following withdrawal of passenger service. Note the incorrect spelling on it. (Lens of Sutton coll.)

90. The former Spring Village goods transfer shed served for storage and workshop purposes. Outside it is Ruston Hornsby no. D2959 of 1955. Its number is ficticious. (P.G.Barnes)

```
         ≷ Day return   02 SEP 97  2nd
0029     Telford (Coalbrookdale)        0029
         to
         Wolverhampton and back

         For conditions see over (M)   1218
```

91. Operating the service was a resident and a visitor. The latter is 0-6-0T no. 662 *Martello* from Bressingham. This is the 10.40 departure from Spring Village. (P.G.Barnes)

92. At the other end of the train was Peckett 0-4-0ST *Rocket*. Working a demonstration freight train is no. 08395, built in 1958 carrying its original number D3429. (P.G.Barnes)

93.   A short length of 2ft gauge track had been laid and on it is this vertical boilered tram engine, which was built by Kirstead in 1979 and named *Thomas* by Revd. W. Awdry. Its engine was from a Victorian launch. (P.G.Barnes)

94.   Brighton line engines were among the few Victorian locomotives to have air brakes; the driver is attending to its compressor. The TSR was reopened to Heath Tunnel on 29th September 2002 and by 2008 the track was in place between Horsehay & Dawley and Doseley, but not fully operational. (P.G.Barnes)

LAWLEY BANK

95. A 1932 northward view has the lamp room (left) remote from the wooden buildings for fire safety reasons. One man could perform all functions here. (R.S.Carpenter coll.)

XVI. The 1927 edition confirms the remote location of the station.

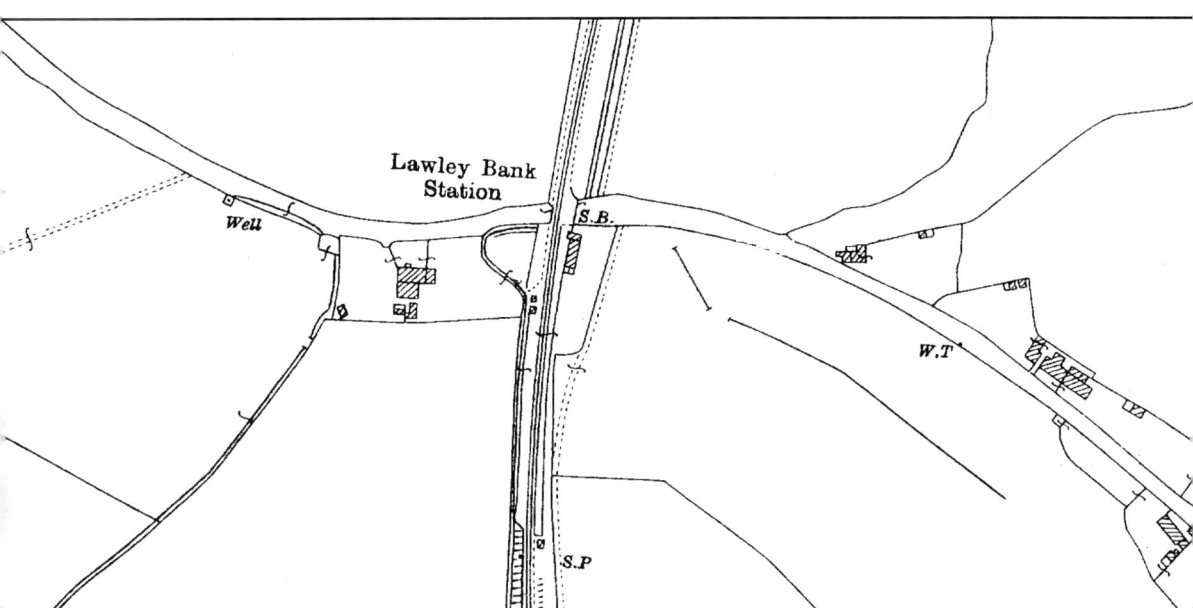

96. North of the station there had been a brickworks with an adit alongside. This drift belonged to the Wrekin Coal Company. This early 1960s picture shows that the lamp hut had been moved onto the platform. (Lens of Sutton coll.)

97. Seen after closure, the station was once noted for the presence of a self-employed porter only 3ft 4ins tall, who used a wheeled orange box to ply his trade. (Lens of Sutton coll.)

NEW DALE HALT

98. The local mining community benefitted from the opening of this halt on 29th January 1934. This area had been scarred by iron and coal workings over a long period. (G.Tilt)

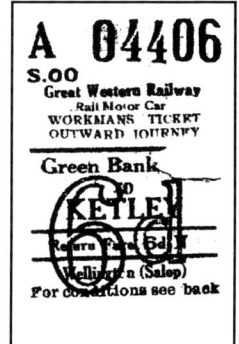

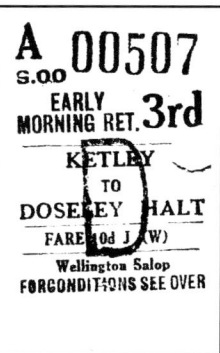

KETLEY TOWN HALT

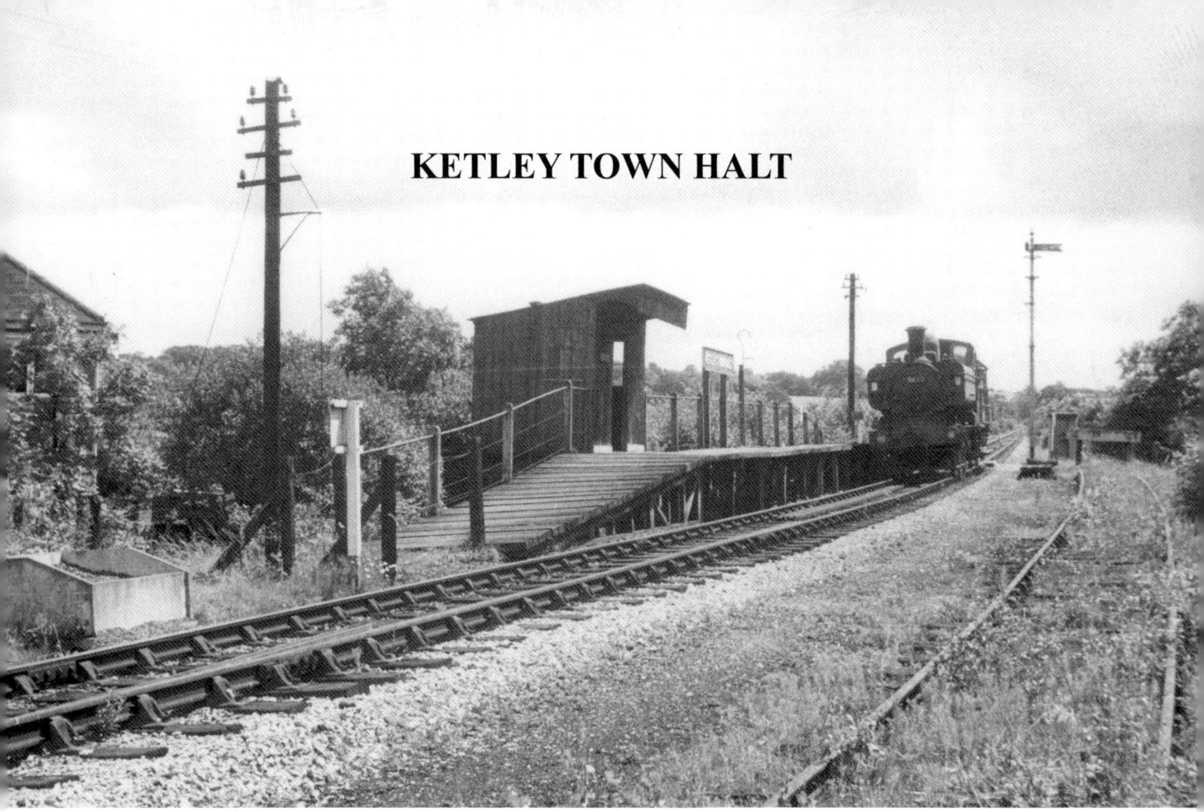

99. Opening on 6th March 1936, this stop served a new residential area called Sinclair Gardens. The siding was the headshunt for a triangular junction to the Sinclair Iron Works. An 0-6-0PT approaches in June 1962. (G.Tilt)

100. Looking north after closure, the shelter has gone and all traffic ceased on 6th July 1964. (Lens of Sutton coll.)

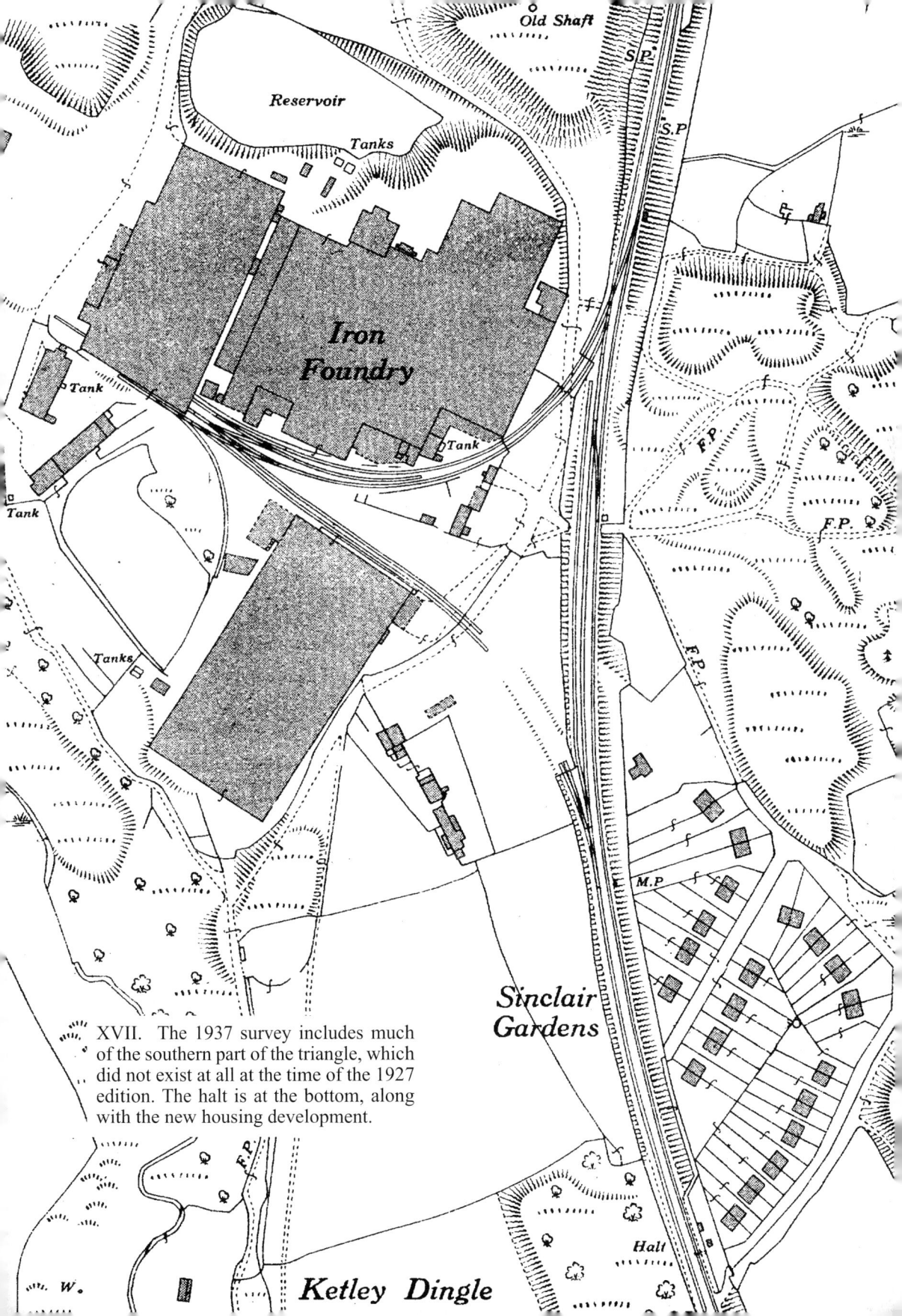

XVII. The 1937 survey includes much of the southern part of the triangle, which did not exist at all at the time of the 1927 edition. The halt is at the bottom, along with the new housing development.

KETLEY

XVIII. The 1902 edition shows the station close to the A5, so numbered in 1919. Ketley Junction is beyond the top left corner.

101. The signal box opened in 1893 and we see another lamp with a dark red warning glass. This postcard is probably from the Edwardian era and reveals the fine barge boards on the station masters house. (Lens of Sutton coll.)

102. The north end of the siding to the Sinclair Iron Company is included in this photograph from August 1932. The goods yard closed on 6th July 1964. (R.M.Casserley coll.)

103. The 3.5pm Wellington to Much Wenlock waits on 5th April 1947; it is headed by 2-6-2T no. 4406. The starting signal and fixed distant are on a wooden post.
(W.A.Camwell/SLS coll.)

➔ 104. A tubular metal signal post was to be seen on 21st June 1962. There had been a siding to the Wrekin Foundry in the centre distance from 1924. From 1947 to 1964 it was used by AGA Heat Co. Ltd. (G.Tilt)

➔ 105. Running north on the same day is 0-6-0PT no. 9636 and it is passing over the A5 trunk road. The shunting of the AGA siding frustrated countless motorists. The line curves through 90° to reach Ketley Junction on the main line. (G.Tilt)

106. An eastward panorama in August 1932 has the turntable on the left, with a locomotive at the coal stage beyond. The buildings and layout date from around 1880.
(Mowat coll./Brunel University)

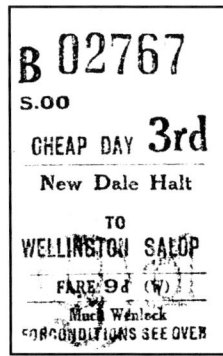

107. Platform 6 was the bay often used by trains to the Coalbrookdale route. No. 4409 is waiting to leave for Craven Arms on 3rd August 1935. The gas lamps are Suggs Windsor pattern. (H.F.Wheeller/R.S.Carpenter coll.)

108. Freight traffic was substantial here, with markets and factories of all types needing transport. Steel and wooden wagons alternate as no. 3749 shunts in 1949. Behind it is No. 2 Box, which was rebuilt in 1953. (D.K.Jones coll.)

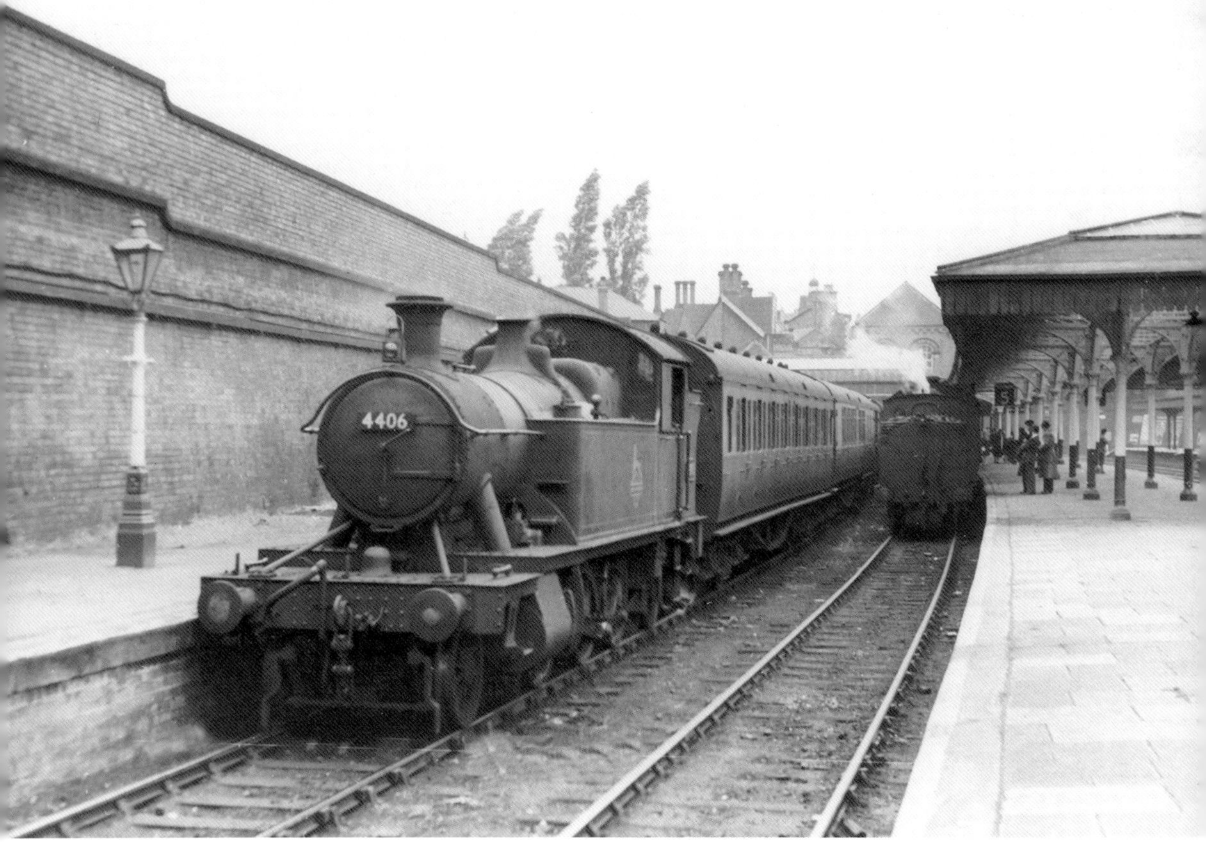

109. No. 4406 is about to work the 4.30pm to Much Wenlock in July 1950. Standing at platform 5 is ex-LNWR 0-6-2T no. 58904 with the 3.53 to Coalport. The main line was always known as the Didcot and Chester route for historical reasons. (T.J.Edgington)

1434
Gt. Western Ry
MONTHLY RETURN
Coalbrookdale to
KETLEY
THIRD CLASS
Fare 1/5 P
Gt Western Ry
MONTHLY
KETLEY to
COALBROOKDALE
THIRD CLASS
Fare 1/5 P
FOR CONDITIONS SEE BACK H.H
1434

3149
3rd-SINGLE SINGLE-3rd
Lawley Bank to
Lawley Bank Lawley Bank
Ketley Ketley
KETLEY
(W) 4d. FARE 4d. (W)
For Conditions see over For Conditions see over
3149

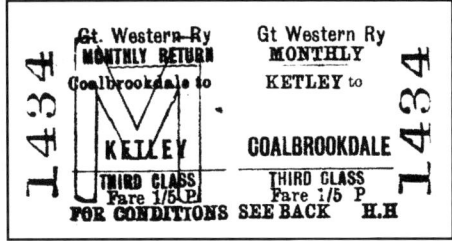

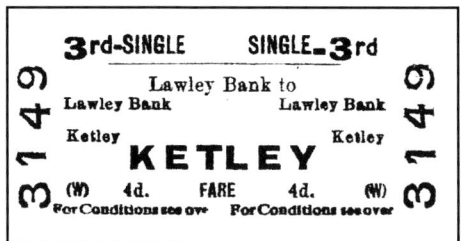

110. An eastward view under Victoria Street bridge includes the ends of the bays and the convergence of the quadruple track. The rods on the left emerge from No.2 Box. (Lens of Sutton coll.)

111. Standing at platform 5 on 7th September 1951 is no. 4401 with the 3.10pm to Craven Arms. The four insulators are where open copper telephone wires change to covered ones. Platform 6 was not used after 8th March 1969. (H.C.Casserley)

112. There were up to ten locomotives allocated here and this view from the mid-1950s includes 2-6-2T no. 5167 and 0-6-0PT no. 5745. In 1934, there were nine 0-6-0s. (R.S.Carpenter)

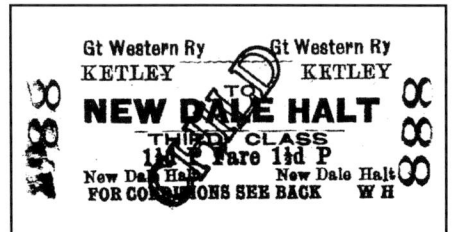

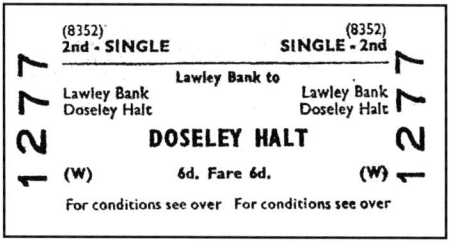

113. Coaling was undertaken in the open in 1957, using a fixed and a mobile crane. The shed seen in picture 106 was followed by one shown in nos 114 and 119. (H.C.Casserley)

114. A 1960 view from platform 3 includes a train on the up loop at platform 1. The through lines once received slip coaches; for example, in the mid-1920s there was one off the 2.10pm from Paddington and another off the 9.10am from Wolverhampton. (R.G.Nelson/T.Walsh)

115. Detail in another 1960 photograph includes a perforated signal post and a water gauge. There were through trains at this time to London, Birkenhead, Stafford, Dover and Bournemouth. (R.G.Nelson/T.Walsh)

116. Seen from the down platform is 2-8-0 no. 3839 and No. 2 box, which had been rebuilt in 1953 to the form seen. It contained the original 71-lever frame and closed on 7th December 2002. Its work was transferred to Madeley Junction box. (P.Q.Treloar coll.)

117. No. 4178 is leaving with the last passenger train to Much Wenlock. It is the 5.45pm on 21st July 1962. On the left are signals for the two bays and the two through lines. (L.W.Rowe)

118. The Winter of 1962-63 was the most severe for generations and few photographs were taken. This features no. 7922 *Salford Hall*, built in 1950 and in store with its chimney covered, its future in question.
(A.J.B.Dodd/P.Chancellor coll.)

➔ 119. A shed survey from 19th August 1963 features no. 9774 taking coal; three tubs are visible. In the background are 2-6-2T no. 41232 and 0-6-0PT no. 9630. The shed closed on 10th August 1964.
(R.Ruffell/M.J.Stretton coll.)

➔ 120. A class 156 DMU runs in from Shrewsbury on 13th May 2002, the last year of semaphore signalling here. The station continued to have four through lines, plus a down bay, numbered 1 and used by an hourly stopping train from Walsall. There was also a basic service of two fast trains per hour, between Birmingham and Shrewsbury or beyond, constituting the most frequent service ever here; it was reduced later. (P.Jones)